I0793460

Eiteljorg Museum

Indianapolis | visit us at **eiteljorg.org**

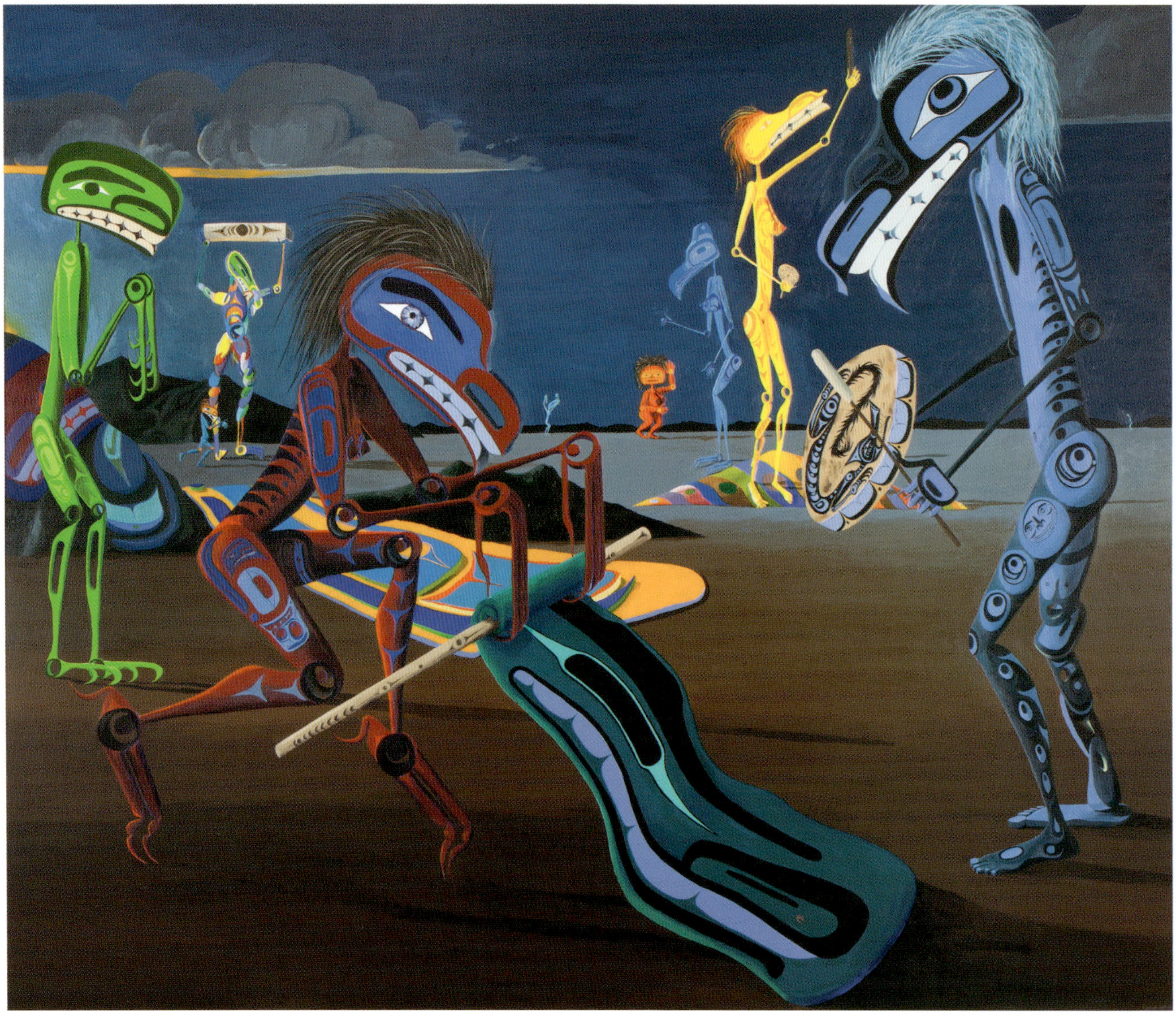

Lawrence Paul Yuxweluptun, *Guardian Spirits on the Land: Ceremony on Sovereignty*, 2000. Acrylic on canvas.

RED

Eiteljorg Contemporary Art Fellowship 2013

Edited by Jennifer Complo McNutt and Ashley Holland (Cherokee)
Eiteljorg Museum of American Indians and Western Art

EITELJORG MUSEUM OF AMERICAN INDIANS AND WESTERN ART
Indianapolis

Library of Congress Cataloging-in-Publication Data

RED (Eiteljorg Museum of American Indians and Western Art)
RED : The Eiteljorg Contemporary Art Fellowship, 2013 / Edited by Jennifer Complo McNutt and Ashley Holland.
pages cm
Includes index.
ISBN 978-0-9798495-7-2 -- ISBN 0-9798495-7-8
1. Indian art--United States--21st century--Exhibitions. 2. Art, American--21st century--Exhibitions. 3. Indian art--Canada--21st century--Exhibitions. 4. Art, Canadian--21st century--Exhibitions. 5. Eiteljorg Museum of American Indians and Western Art--Funds and scholarships. I. McNutt, Jennifer Complo, editor of compilation. II. Holland, Ashley (Ashley R.), 1983- editor of compilation. III. Eiteljorg Museum of American Indians and Western Art. IV. Title.
N6538.A4R43 2013
704.03'97007477252--dc23
2013035818

Eiteljorg Museum of American Indians and Western Art, 500 W. Washington Street, Indianapolis, IN 46204, U.S.A., (317) 636-9378; http://www.eiteljorg.org

Editorial services and project management by Suzanne G. Fox, Red Bird Publishing, Inc., Bozeman, Montana
Editing by Jean Christensen, Arlington, Virginia
Graphic design by Steve Sipe, Director of Exhibit and Graphic Design, Eiteljorg Museum
Indexing by Sherry L. Smith, Bend, Oregon
Proofreading by Jane Jacobi, Clemson, South Carolina

Unless otherwise cited, all photographs are by Dirk Bakker, Artbook, Huntington Woods, Michigan, or Tad Fruits, Brownsburg, Indiana.

Front and back cover illustration: Lawrence Paul Yuxweluptun, *Portrait of a Residential School Child,* 2005. Acrylic on canvas.

Special thanks to the following sponsors for their generous support of *RED*: Eiteljorg Contemporary Art Fellowship.

PRESENTED BY

Lilly Endowment Inc.

SPONSORED BY

BMO Private Bank

Christel DeHaan Family Foundation,
in honor of the children and families of Christel House
David H. & Barbara M. Jacobs Foundation
David Jacobs
The Ed Klink Emerging Artist Fund
Gerald and Dorit Paul

IN-KIND SUPPORT

Sun King Brewing Company

Contents

Foreword

We are excited to share with you the eighth biennial presentation of the Eiteljorg Contemporary Art Fellowship. Launched in 1999, the Fellowship program recognizes the work of emerging and established Native American and First Nations artists working with contemporary media and ideas. Broadly speaking, the mission is to raise awareness of this art and honor its makers. Specifically, we select five artists to be spotlighted in each cycle with a major group exhibition and publication. Each artist receives an unrestricted fellowship award of $25,000. We recognize these artists during a celebratory weekend in Indianapolis that includes a symposium of presentations and conversation. Furthermore, the museum acquires representative works from each artist for its permanent collection.

In June 2014, the Eiteljorg Museum will celebrate its 25th anniversary. This will be a special time for commemoration and reflection. On this silver anniversary, as we stand back to assess our accomplishments and challenges and dream of what the future holds, nothing will be more important than the Eiteljorg Contemporary Art Fellowship.

Here are some numbers to help us understand the impact of the Fellowship initiative. To date, forty-five artists have been awarded Eiteljorg Fellowships, an extraordinary cohort representing the foremost in Native contemporary art. More than fifty Native and non-Native authors have contributed to eight publications that have been distributed to national and international audiences.

The amount of money the program has generated in direct support for Native artists is significant, and its impact is even greater. Artists have received a total of $1,125,000 in fellowships to further their art through equipment, travel, research, and greater financial stability. Another $250,000 has been invested to publish their art along with essays from leading thinkers to encourage the continued documentation and dialogue about Native art. More than $900,000 has been allocated to purchase works for the Eiteljorg's permanent collection for future generations to view, study, and draw inspiration from. These accomplishments will help Native contemporary artists leave a legacy for future artists and for audiences, and will enhance the greater understanding and appreciation of indigenous people in the twentieth and twenty-first centuries.

Numbers are revealing and help us assess our position in the field; they express our high level of commitment and outreach. However, the program is about people. I have always said the heart of the program is contained in the title "fellowship," the coming together of people—the artists, scholars, curators, collectors, and the public. The relationships among these people may begin (or in some cases, existing ones are nurtured) during the gathering in Indianapolis, but the fellowship among these colleagues continues for a lifetime.

Since the Eiteljorg Museum's inauguration in 1989, it has been important for the museum to be a platform for Native expressions of all forms. The Fellowship program is a significant part of that successful effort. Sustaining and continuing the program are made possible by a great many people and organizations to which we owe a debt of gratitude. First, I want to recognize the leadership of Jennifer Complo-McNutt, the Eiteljorg's curator of contemporary art, who has shepherded the project since its inception, along with our assistant curator, Ashley Holland. They have done a wonderful job these past two years of bringing the project to completion. I also want to thank James Nottage, Vice President, Chief Curatorial Officer and Gund Curator of Western Art, for his support and in particular his management of this publication.

Once again, I want you to know that the Eiteljorg Contemporary Art Fellowship would not be possible without the extraordinary support provided by the Lilly Endowment. The endowment supported our goal to raise the public's awareness of Native American contemporary art when we began the program sixteen years ago, and it continues to do so. The Lilly Endowment has provided an unprecedented base of support totaling more than $3,500,000 for the Fellowship program, allowing the museum to continue and expand this important work.

I want to offer a special thank you to longtime museum supporters and contemporary art collectors Gerald and Dorit Paul for their generous support. We are also indebted to the Christel DeHaan Family Foundation, in honor of the children and families of Christel House, which provided a major grant for the project. Additionally, we are pleased to recognize the Transformation Trust for providing funds to create the Ed Klink Emerging Artists' Fund. We also thank David H. Jacobs for his ongoing support of this project. The impact of these philanthropic gifts cannot be overstated. Thank you all.

In May 2012, the Fellowship exhibition traveled outside the walls of the museum for the first time. The exhibition *We Are Here* opened at the Smithsonian Institution's National Museum of the American Indian's George Gustav Heye Center in New York City. I want to recognize the leadership of the Heye Center's director, John Haworth, along with NMAI director Kevin Gover, for supporting this collaboration. I also want to thank The Efroymson Fund of the Central Indiana Community Foundation for supporting the Eiteljorg's participation.

We also owe a debt of gratitude to the collectors who have generously loaned their artworks to support the exhibition. Of special note are Michael O'Brian and other private collectors, who have generously shared significant portions of their collections of Lawrence Paul Yuxweluptun's work. Yuxweluptun is a prolific artist with many avid collectors, and we are pleased to have their loans as part of this exhibition. We are grateful to Sarah E. Macaulay of Macaulay & Co. Fine Art, who also loaned works by Yuxweluptun. Julie Buffalohead's work is represented by loans from the National Museum of the American Indian and many individuals, and we are grateful for the assistance of Todd Bockley of the Bockley Gallery in Minneapolis. Loans have come from as far away as Homer, Alaska and the Pratt Museum for Nicholas Galanin. Works by Shan Goshorn have come from the Minneapolis Institute of Arts, the National Museum of the American Indian, the Fred Jones Jr. Museum at the University of Oklahoma, and many other individual collectors.

We are proud to present this latest edition of the *Eiteljorg Contemporary Art Fellowship*, and hope you will be inspired, provoked, and amazed.

John Vanausdall, President and Chief Executive Officer
Eiteljorg Museum of American Indians and Western Art

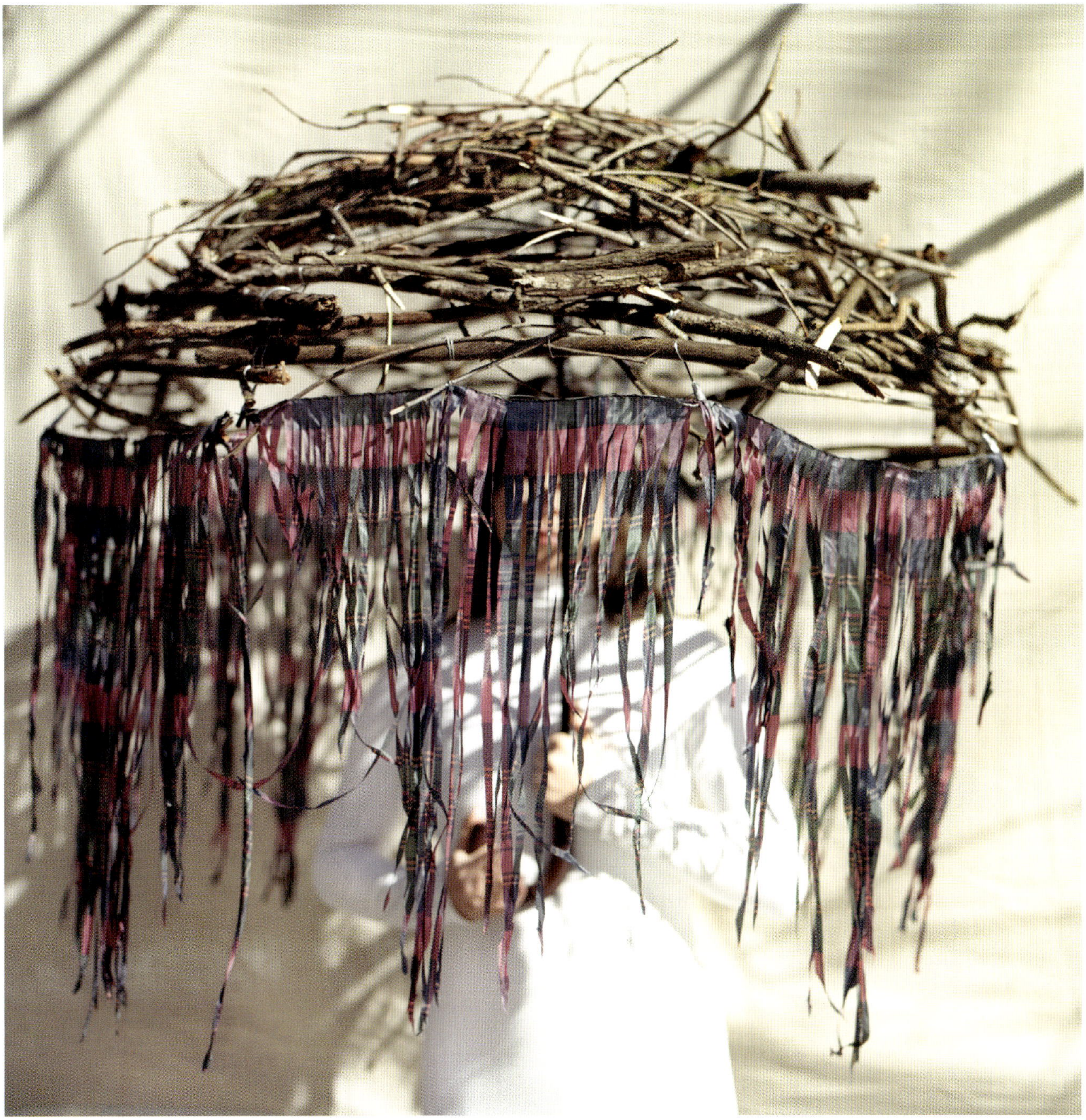

Meryl McMaster, *Caduceus (In-Between Worlds series)*, 2010. Digital chromogenic print. Image courtesy the artist.

The Power of **RED**

Ashley Holland (Cherokee), Assistant Curator of Contemporary Art, and Jennifer Complo McNutt, Curator of Contemporary Art
Eiteljorg Museum of American Indians and Western Art

Choosing a title for any exhibition and book can be a struggle. Most projects begin with a theme or the examination of a particular artist, and title selection soon becomes obvious. The situation is reversed for the *Eiteljorg Contemporary Art Fellowship*. Only after the artists are chosen and the work is selected can the title be determined. The title shapes the way visitors view the show, defines the image of the accompanying catalogue, and becomes the verbal identity of the project.

Despite what Shakespeare stated in Juliet's famous musings on a rose, a name, or in this case an exhibition title, is not just a title. It is a large part of a project's identity. The trick is to find a title that projects the power of the exhibition and the artists it represents as a whole.

The title of the eighth round of the Eiteljorg Contemporary Art Fellowship is *RED*. When we decided on the name, we discussed what it meant. Words like "resistance," "resilience," "education," "dialogue," and "earth" were tossed around to see if they fit or would add to the overall idea of *RED*. We decided that *RED* by itself embodied the strength, drama, determination, and humor of the art and the artists. It is the color of power. It is symbolic of blood, the essence of life that keeps our bodies functioning. It declares that any person who lives with the idea that Native people are vanishing, weak, or failing to thrive needs simply to look at their art.

It makes sense that choosing the title for the biennial *Eiteljorg Contemporary Art Fellowship* exhibition must wait until the artists are selected through a rigorous adjudication process by an independent group of art experts. This group typically includes a previous Fellow, a member of the Native art field, and a notable figure from the larger world of contemporary art. Special thanks go to the 2013 Fellowship selection committee: Bonnie Devine (Ojibwa), Melissa Bob (Lummi), and Lisa Freiman.[1] Their task was to choose the Fellows by viewing images of art made by each artist who had been nominated or had applied for a fellowship. The works the committee views do not necessarily end up in the exhibition. Once the artists are identified, the curator of contemporary art selects pieces for the show that she views during interviews at the artists' studios and sometimes at other museums and the homes of collectors. Themes and ideas for the show and its title emerge from this process, which is creative and time-consuming. The results are worth the journey.

RED features five Fellows who exemplify the highest standards of artistic excellence in the field of Native contemporary art. These artists represent unique cultural and personal backgrounds, and their artwork reflects the diversity of Native artists in North America. The combination of paintings, drawings, photography, sculpture, and installation art once again proves that there is no such thing as stereotypical Native art. The works show clearly that a range of media and voices demonstrates the true power of *RED*. Many of the works come from tradition layered in contemporary experiences and transformed with new media and unique nontraditional materials, while others express the reinvention of traditional arts.

This year's invited artist, who does not have to apply for the Fellowship and is selected by the committee, is Lawrence Paul Yuxweluptun (Coast Salish/Okanagan) of Canada, an obvious choice to join the illustrious group of previous Fellowship exhibition headliners.[2] Few Native artists are as prolific as Yuxweluptun. His work beautifully, and often sardonically, encompasses the political and social issues that inform Native artists.

I work for art, not to be used by racism. I make art to get rid of racism. I am concerned with the colonial mentality that is directly responsible for the killing of wolves, buffalo, whales, grizzly bears, and migratory birds, to the point that some species are now extinct. It is behind the depletion of fish stocks on the west and east coasts, acid rain, nuclear waste, landfills, smog, the greenhouse effect, the emission of methane gas, mining tailings, endangered animals, pollution of freshwater reservoirs, toxic wastes of all kinds, oil spills, uranium mining, nuclear testing. The next step

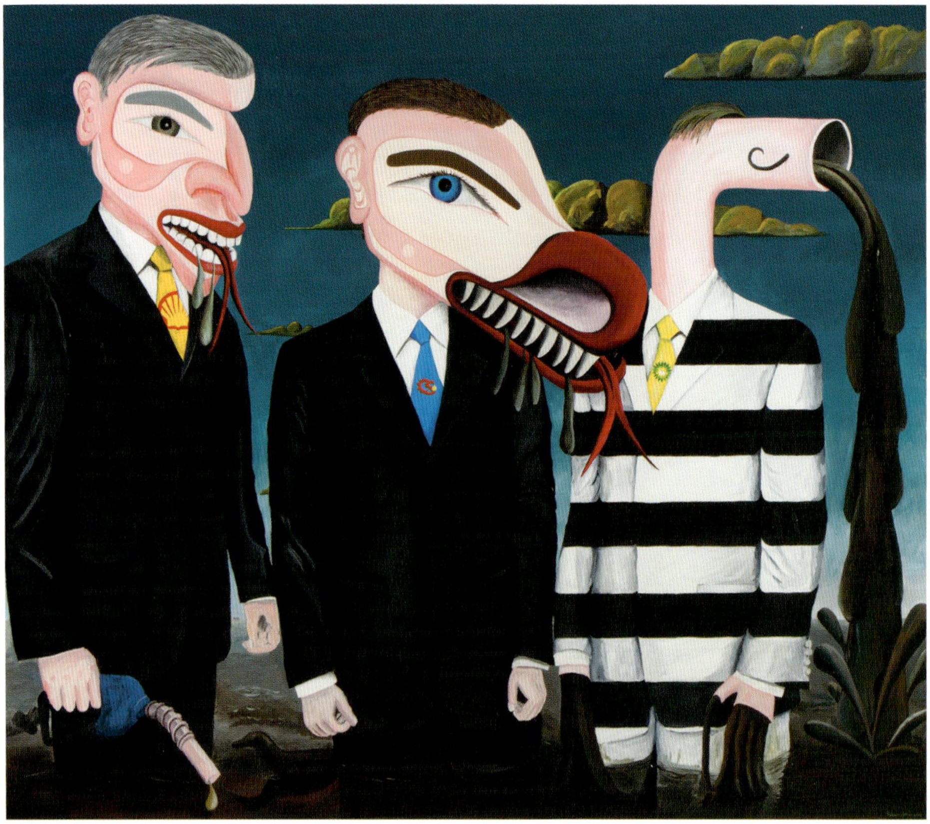

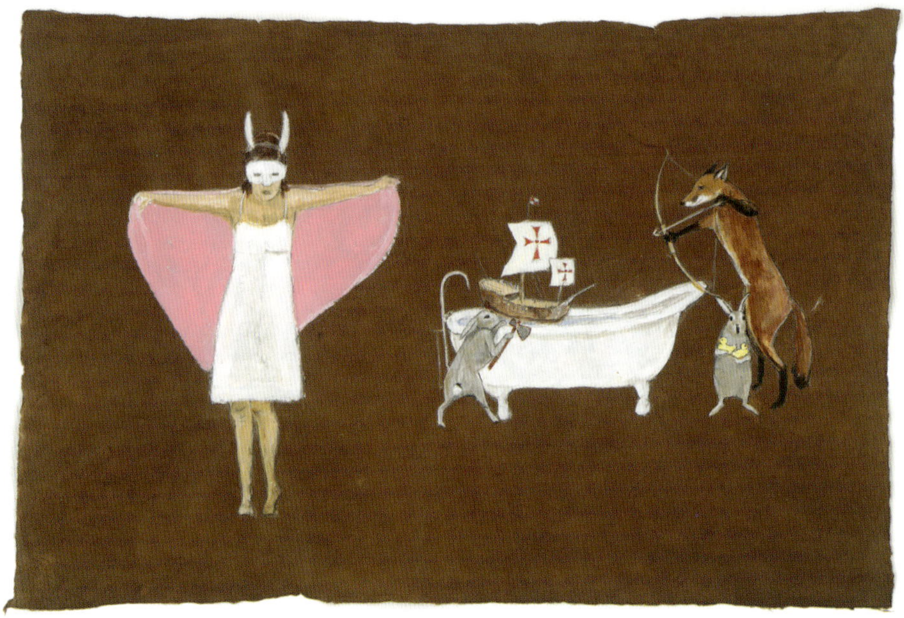

(Above) Lawrence Paul Yuxweluptun, *Fucking Creeps They're Environmental Terrorists*, 2013. Acrylic on canvas. (Below) Julie Buffalohead, *The Columbus Prophecies*, 2012. Mixed media on paper. Image courtesy the Bockley Gallery.

towards de-colonization of First Nations must be recognition by the provincial governments of our sovereign indigenous government. As sovereign caretakers of the land, our forebears were always the protectors of the biosphere.[3]

It is easy to get lost in the beauty of his surrealist landscapes or to be amused by the politicians in works such as *Fucking Creeps They're Environmental Terrorists*. His humor does not release the offending parties from Yuxweluptun's demand for land rights and environmental preservation.

Two-dimensional work dominates the 2013 Eiteljorg Fellowship. Our second artist working in this format is Julie Buffalohead (Ponca Tribe of Oklahoma). She is a painter, papermaker, mother of one, and wife. Her quiet demeanor belies the passions of her deeply personal work. The perceptive viewer sees depictions of Buffalohead's myths, fairy tales, humor, hopes, and haunting fears. These are delicate images on fine, hand-crafted paper that evoke subtle but powerful emotions.

My recent series reflects a journey of a more personal nature. The narrative tension my work creates emanates from the Native oral tradition of storytelling, while I blend in my own distinct strands of make-believe.[4]

She has noted further:

My imagery is so personal it's hard to think about the viewer, but I try to be provocative. I use stereotypes because Indians didn't have a hand in creating them. It's my way of saying, "This is not who we are. This is your invention.[5]

The Columbus Prophesies exemplifies the mythical history that society has created and continues to endure. Buffalohead creates this piece to revise that history, and she is punitive in her actions toward the offenders.

Nicholas Galanin (Tlingit/Aleut) is a Sitka, Alaska-based artist and musician who completed his studies in London and New Zealand. His artwork shifts from music to art, to his musical alter ego, Silver Jackson, and back, to the expressions of a Native artist protesting the past and professing his confidence in defining and depicting his future. Galanin states:

Culture cannot be contained as it unfolds. My art enters this stream at many different points, looking backwards, looking forwards, generating its own sound and motion. I am inspired by generations of Tlingit creativity and contribute to this wealthy conversation through active curiosity. There is no room in this exploration for the tired prescriptions of the "Indian Art World" and its institutions. Through creating, I assert my freedom.[6]

An example of that freedom is found in work such as *The American Dream is a Alie and Well* that initially appears as a physical representation of the American Dream and of power and strength through its use of the American flag and bullets. However, one simply has to look at the title to realize the artist's meaning. The American dream is not a truth for everyone.

Shan Goshorn (Eastern Band of Cherokee) is from Tulsa, Oklahoma, and originally trained as a painter and photographer. She now embraces the traditional practice of Cherokee basket weaving with decidedly contemporary techniques and messages. Her intricate baskets are inspiring and truly the work of a Native artist taking a traditional form and giving it a contemporary and political twist.

I strive to educate an audience about some of the unique issues that continue to impact Indian people.... Whether it is from the attempts to erase all Native identity by denying Indian children their language and culture through boarding schools assimilation, breaking ties among tribal supports through Indian relocation acts, providing Indian people with commodity foods that have contributed to major illnesses, etc., historical trauma continues to plague us in a big way. It is my goal to enlighten audiences to these ongoing practices and encourage honest dialogue between people.[7]

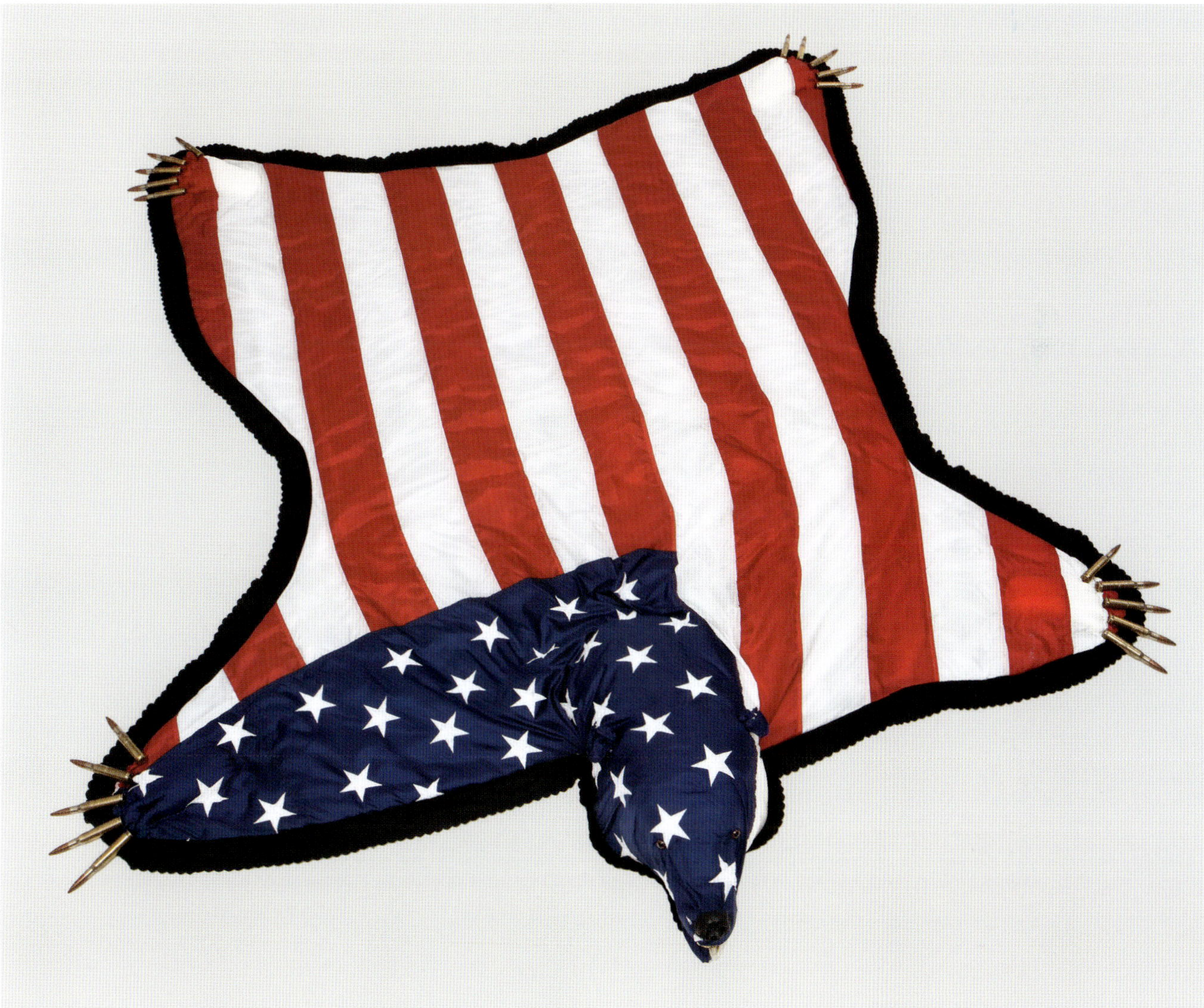

Nicholas Galanin, *The American Dream is Alie and Well*, 2012. United States flag, felt, .50 caliber blank cartridges, foam, gold leaf, plastic.

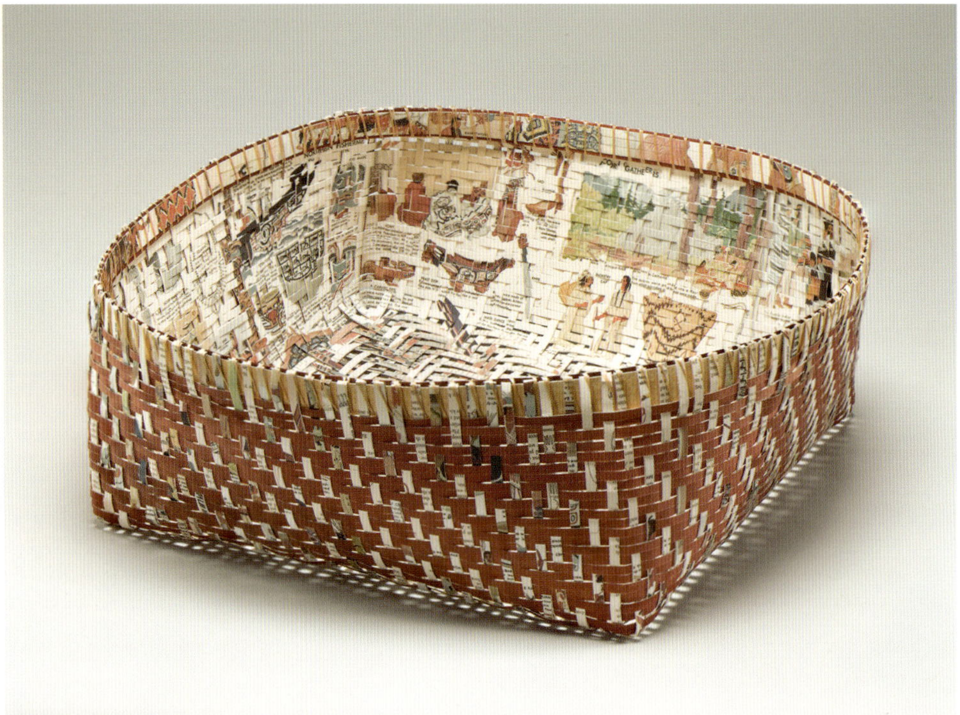

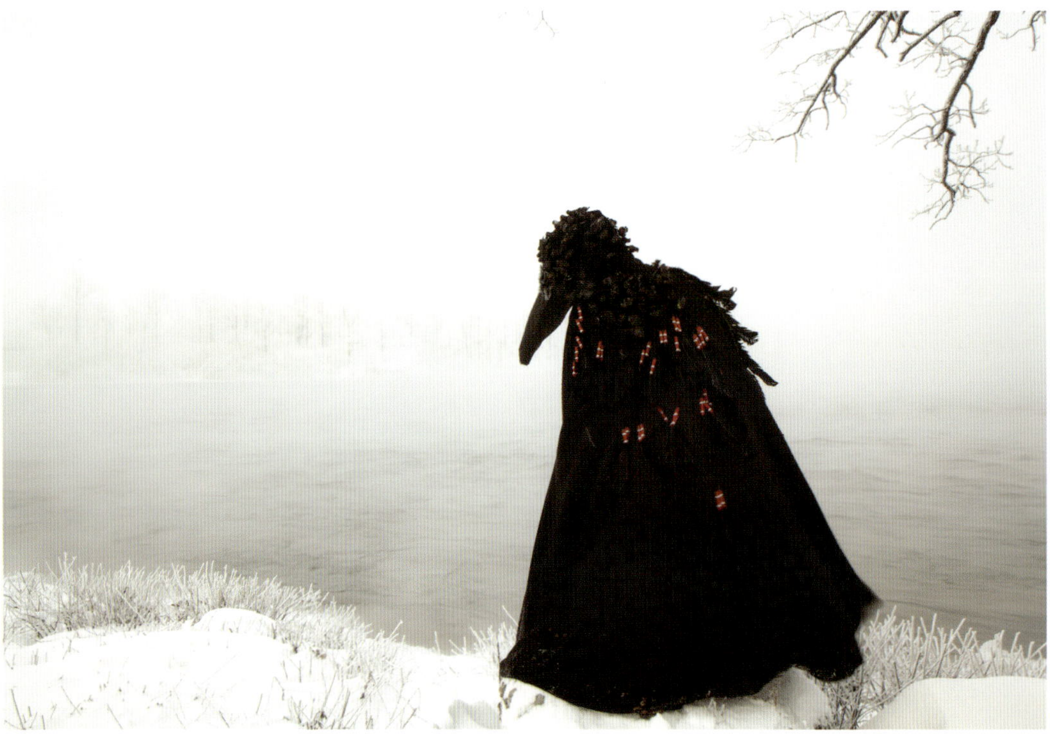

(Above) Shan Goshorn, *Separating the Chaff*, 2013. Archival watercolor paper splints, first printed with archival inks. (Below) Meryl McMaster, *Wingeds Calling (In-Between Worlds series)*, 2012. Digital chromogenic print. Image courtesy the artist.

As an example of this melding of tradition and social conscience, the traditional single-weave basket created in a winnowing or sifter style titled *Separating the Chaff* was created not from sweetgrass and river cane, but from the deconstructed image of an encyclopedia page from the 1960s and a book on Indians from 1956. The work is about filtering what America thinks it knows about Native people.

Meryl McMaster (Plains Cree/Blackfoot) is a young artist from Ottawa, Ontario, whose work shows a maturity in its beauty and simplicity and its contradictions of Native experiences.

My artistic practice begins with photography evoking a journey that follows a path of self-discovery. It goes beyond straight photography by incorporating manual production, performance, and self-reflection. My work unravels notions of identity and subjectivity as something that is never complete, but always in process and always formed from within.[8]

McMaster's series *In-Between Worlds* truly embodies this ideal of a journey to self-reflection. Her use of handmade props and haunting locales results in visually rich images. McMaster's work will resonate in the memory of its audience.

McMaster's unique exposure to contemporary Native and especially First Nations art lies in the fact that she is the daughter of author and curator Gerald McMaster, who was in the first group of selectors (1999) and helped forge the format for the Eiteljorg Contemporary Art Fellowship. In the first Fellowship catalogue, Gerald McMaster stated:

Aboriginal contemporary art, by its very nature, is work being done today, for today, and about today. Artists borrow from everywhere. They look at ancient images, forms, and techniques, with an understanding that what their ancestors had to say continues to have meaning for them, and us all, in the present. None of them wishes us to believe they are located in some mythic past; instead, they understand their realities as energetic practices of today, which offer them an unparalleled range within which to express themselves.[9]

Gerald McMaster made this statement almost fifteen years ago, and its truth still holds. The 2013 Fellows embody the meaning of *RED* in this context. As an exhibition, *RED* is a platform for exploring the work of artists who take pride in their cultures and express strength in the knowledge that has been passed down from their ancestors. It is the idea of self-identity and personal reflection. *RED* demonstrates contemporary expression informed by millennia of knowledge and experience. Art of the 2013 Fellows is, indeed, about power and life and the present.

---

[1]Melissa Bob was formerly with Crow's Shadow Institute of the Arts and currently is the director of community development for Children's Mental Health & Youth Engagement at the National Indian Child Welfare Association (NICWA). Bonnie Devine was a 2011 Eiteljorg Fellow and is a professor at Ontario College of Art & Design, Toronto. Lisa Freiman was the former senior curator of contemporary art at the Indianapolis Museum of Art and currently is the director of the Institute of Contemporary Art at Virginia Commonwealth University, Richmond.

[2]Previous leading artists for the Fellowship program, from 1999 through 2011, have been George Morrison, Allan Houser, Kay WalkingStick, John Hoover, James Luna, Edward Poitras, and Alan Michelson.

[3]"Lawrence Paul Yuxweluptun: Biography and Discussion," created July 28, 2008, http://voices.yahoo.com/lawrence-paul-yuxweluptun-biography-discussion-1708377.html.

[4]Julie Buffalohead, artist's statement for Eiteljorg Museum, 2012.

[5]"Julie Buffalohead," Bockley Gallery, accessed June 5, 2013, http://bockleygallery.com/artist_buffalohead/index.html.

[6]Nicholas Galanin, artist's statement for Eiteljorg Museum, 2012.

[7]Shan Goshorn, artist's statement for Eiteljorg Museum, 2012.

[8]Meryl McMaster, artist's statement for Eiteljorg Museum, 2012.

[9]Quoted in Bruce Bernstein, "Philosophies, Histories, Identities," *Contemporary Masters, The Eiteljorg Fellowship for Native American Fine Art* (Indianapolis: Eiteljorg Museum of American Indians and Western Art, 1999), 6.

RED

Eiteljorg Contemporary Art Fellowship 2013

Lawrence Paul Yuxweluptun
(Coast Salish/Okanagan)

Julie Buffalohead
(Ponca Tribe of Oklahoma)

Nicholas Galanin
(Tlingit/Aleut)

Shan Goshorn
(Eastern Band of Cherokee)

Meryl McMaster
(Plains Cree/Blackfoot)

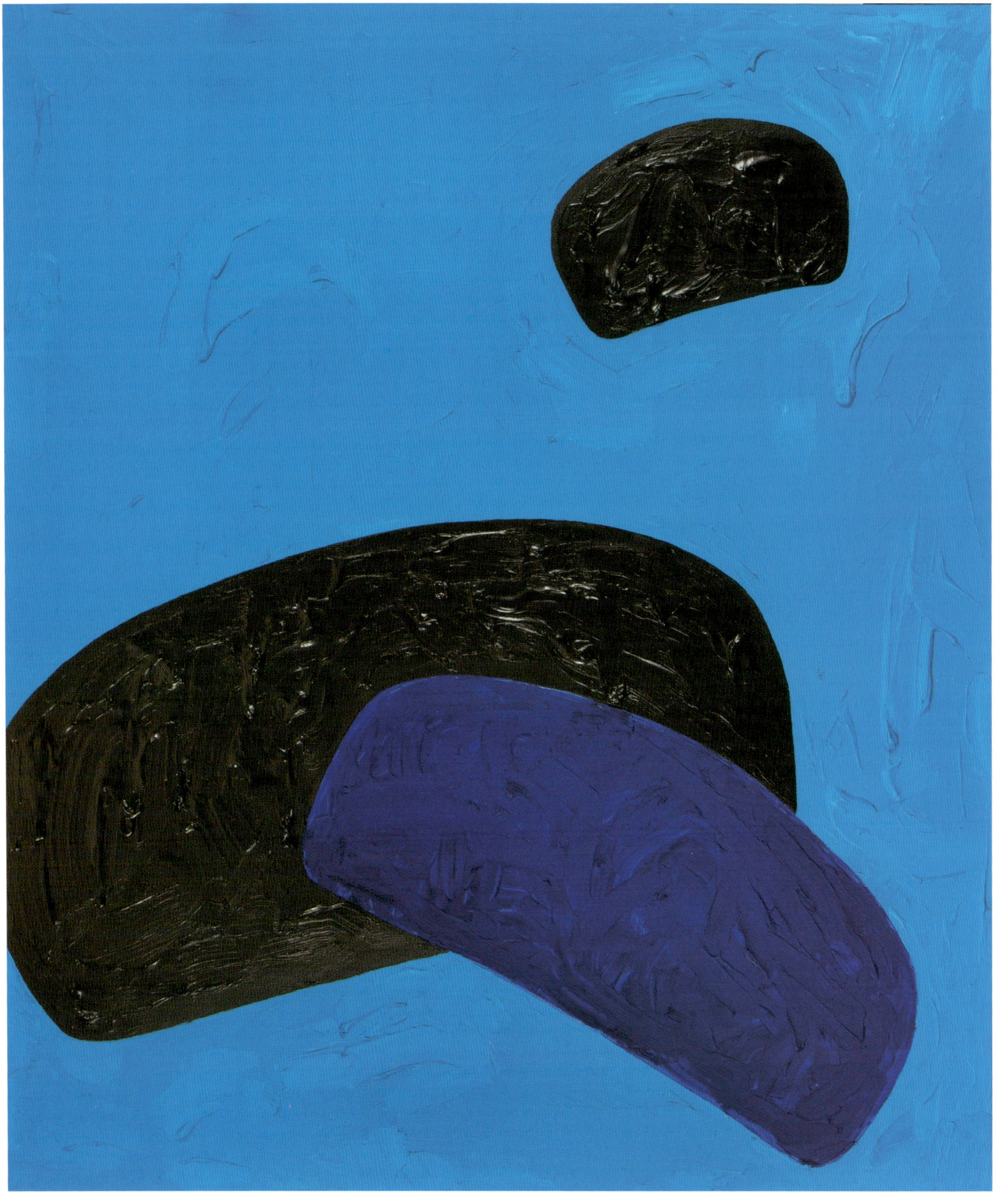

Black Ovoids in Deep Blue Sea, 2013. Acrylic on canvas.

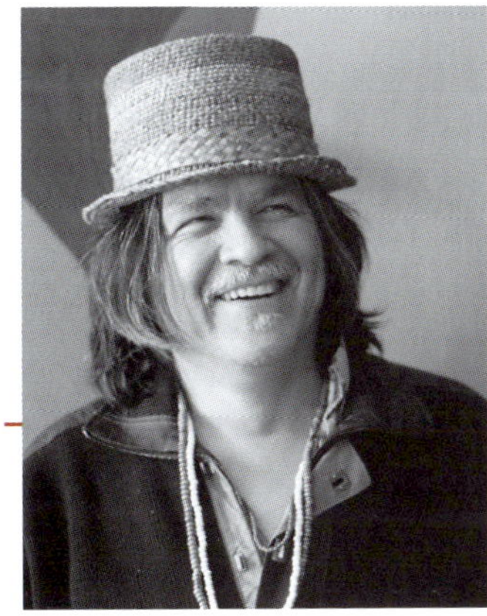

Lawrence Paul Yuxweluptun

(Coast Salish/Okanagan)

Master Mixer, Man of Many Colors

Dana Claxton (Lakota)

I work for art, not to be used by racism. I make art to get rid of racism.

Lawrence Paul Yuxweluptun has been drawing and painting since he could hold an instrument in his hand. He once stated, "The paintbrush is like a weapon," and in his case, it is a weapon against the pen and the written word that colonialists used to dehumanize indigenous people and to steal Indian land. He has also stated, "I am a history painter." For over thirty years, he has been painting the "Indian" condition and all the complexities of being Indian, past, present, and future. He paints land...Indian land. The indigenous imperative to honor land has fueled most of his artistic output for the last three decades. And within the honoring of land, he weaves indigenous sovereignty and the de-subjugation and humanization of indigenous bodies right into the living land herself.[1]

Of Salish and Okanagan descent, Yuxweluptun attended residential school for two years and then was among the first generation of Indigenous people in Canada to attend public school. On his first day of public school, his white friend from the neighborhood asked, "Why are you walking to school with us?" Lawrence replied, "They changed the laws. We can go to public schools now." Later when he returned home, he asked his dad, "Why are there no graveyards [at this school]?" And his dad answered, "There are no graveyards at public school."[2]

Yuxweluptun has declared that "Canada is like a baby crawling around wearing a dirty diaper," suggesting that the nation is in an immature state of being and needs to come clean of its insidious past of legally oppressing Indians and the continued denial that there is anything wrong with the current state of aboriginal people. The bonds between Indian and non-Indian peoples are complex, filled with love, hate, desire, confusion, distrust, and fear. Canada and the United States have difficult histories that have shaped the difficult present. It is not always a pleasant picture, but Yuxweluptun vividly paints large-scale paintings and makes etchings, drawings, performances, installations, and sculptures that often depict these realities. His work addresses land use, land claims, and land spirits while always steadfastly stating that land is alive and needs to be respected and nurtured, cared for, loved. His work is shaped by indigenous imperatives of walking gently on the earth and not doing too much damage. His body of work has persuaded viewers to love Mother Earth and perhaps even love Indian people. He has often asked audiences, "Can you love Indian people?"[3]

He is a history painter on high alert, always questioning and probing what damage is being inflicted upon the Earth as well as to indigenous people. Considering the erosions of the Earth and indigenous rights and cultural traditions, he has followed up his now-infamous painting *Redman Watching White Man Fix Hole in Sky* with works that consider the corporatization of the Earth. He paints the mostly male corporate cast as eco-destroyers. Perhaps the most racist, sexist act of all is the killing of Mother, who indigenous people have been saying since time immemorial commands respect. Misogyny meets xenophobia—the killing of Mother Earth is the killing of indigenous worldviews. With all the extractions that are mined from her, one would think our shared humanity could alleviate poverty. A fellow indigenous leader and one of Yuxweluptun's heroes, Sitting Bull, said in 1885, "The white man knows how to make everything, but does not know how to distribute it."[4]

Yuxweluptun's art is about listening to the songbirds and constitutes a plea to care for the land and to recognize indigenous land rights. Via the exhibition of his art in public museums, his paintings have demanded from the viewer, the curator, the art historian, the educator, and the student that they consider indigenous rights and worldviews. Aside from the historical context, he places indigenous concerns front and center in contemporary life within his art.

Painting, the most primitive of the arts, consists of humans marking on surfaces to render themselves.[5] And through the evolution from marking on cave walls to painting on canvas, Yuxweluptun—as "natural man"—takes this art form and renders his Native self, along with his concerns as a Native man. As he paints, the landscape comes alive through vivid colors of faces, eyes, and hands within the land. He paints faces on clouds and inside tree branches and renders trees as living beings whom he considers his relatives. The mighty cedar trees of the Northwest Coast are his cousins and old uncles and aunties. From oil spills, to holes in the sky, to the spirit of the land, he relentlessly paints to acknowledge the Earth's being. Who speaks for Mother Earth? Yuxweluptun does.

Yuxweluptun has his own original style, and the nexus is his Salish culture, combined and layered with his training and honors in painting. He has taken his cultural identity, worldview, and Northwest Coast iconography and painted the canvas. He is a warrior artist painting the Indian landscape, which is rich in spirit. Hopi scholar and filmmaker Victor Masayesva has stated, "Indigenous culture—not popular culture—will continue to dominate the North American continent as the clearest manifestation of its soul."[6] Time and time again, this has played out in visual art. It has been well documented how western art movements have borrowed from indigenous cultures. Andrea Breton and the surrealists were interested in the shape-shifter masks of the Northwest Coast, Cubism borrowed from African sculpture, modernism attempted (and failed) to realize utopian ideals for which North American tribal communities were well known, and abstract expressionism claimed the philosophy of indigenous freedom, which is about having the freedom to be an individual within the tribe without being individualistic.[7] And certainly fashion has expropriated indigenous motifs, from the 1920s Indian Princess to the hippy fringe and back-to-the-earth movement of the 1960s, to the recent exploited Navajo geometrics splattered over everything from underwear to luxury bath towels. Indigenous and tribal aesthetics haunt the western world, but such uses ignore the real living people, with real lives and real problems. In some indigenous communities, there is a state of emergency regarding language extinctions, suicides, poverty, and substance abuse. This is true about the violence toward aboriginal women, youth, and men who have been structurally dehumanized by the state and church and through education and popular culture. How can indigenous people value themselves or be valued under this tyranny? These concerns are part of

Yuxweluptun's everyday existence. His titles often reveal what he is thinking about current Indian affairs.

The Americas are not a European country—they are Indian. This is the continent of the Indian, and the soul of this continent is indigenous. Yuxweluptun continues to place aboriginal existence and imperatives at the center of his artistic output with the hope that the viewer will embrace the philosophy that caring for Mother Earth and her stewardship is our collective responsibility. This is the importance of his significant practice within contemporary Native American art-making, along with inspiring generations of young painters and artists to make art that has the deep meaning, conviction, and purpose of his own work.

The Salish and other Northwest Coast tribal groups have cultural iconographies and forms that are distinct to the region: the split u, u form, and ovoid, among others. As an artist of Salish lineage, Yuxweluptun has placed these ancient forms in acrylic paintings, drawings, and prints. The ancient forms become contemporary cultural signifiers of the Northwest Coast formline. In some cases, he has isolated the ovoid while maintaining the lineage, sometimes through traditional coastal colors of red, black, and white, which were all gathered from the land. Black can be gathered by crushing a wasp's nest with bear grease, red from the red stone, and white from crushing clam shells. In Yuxweluptun's painting, there is an explosion of color on the canvas. He renders these ancient forms on canvas, and they are placed onto the gallery wall—the new cave. The gallery space for artists of all cultural backgrounds is a place to make sense of the world around us.

Yuxweluptun moves fluidly from large scale to intimate works, from color to black and white. Thirty-one works are included in this exhibition, ranging from large-scale paintings in acrylic on canvas to intimate drawings and prints. The range of scale and hue and everything in between significantly represents his extensive *oeuvre*, moving with ease from one medium and scale to the other. Whether abstract or his unique blend of Northwest Coast Salish surrealism, all the paintings maintain a color range that he invents. As a master mixer colorist, his palette refuses to remain the same after all these years of painting.

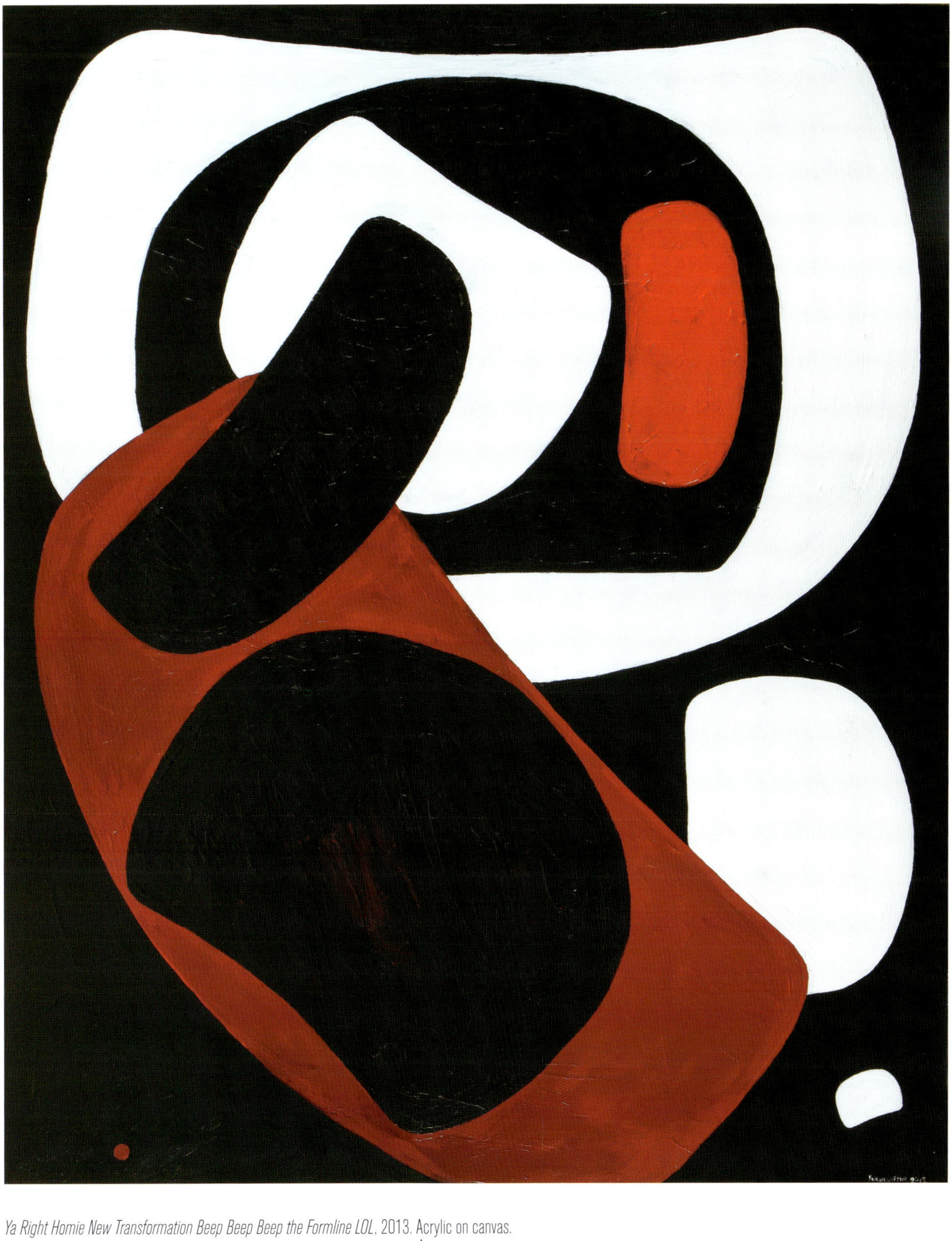

Ya Right Homie New Transformation Beep Beep Beep the Formline LOL, 2013. Acrylic on canvas.

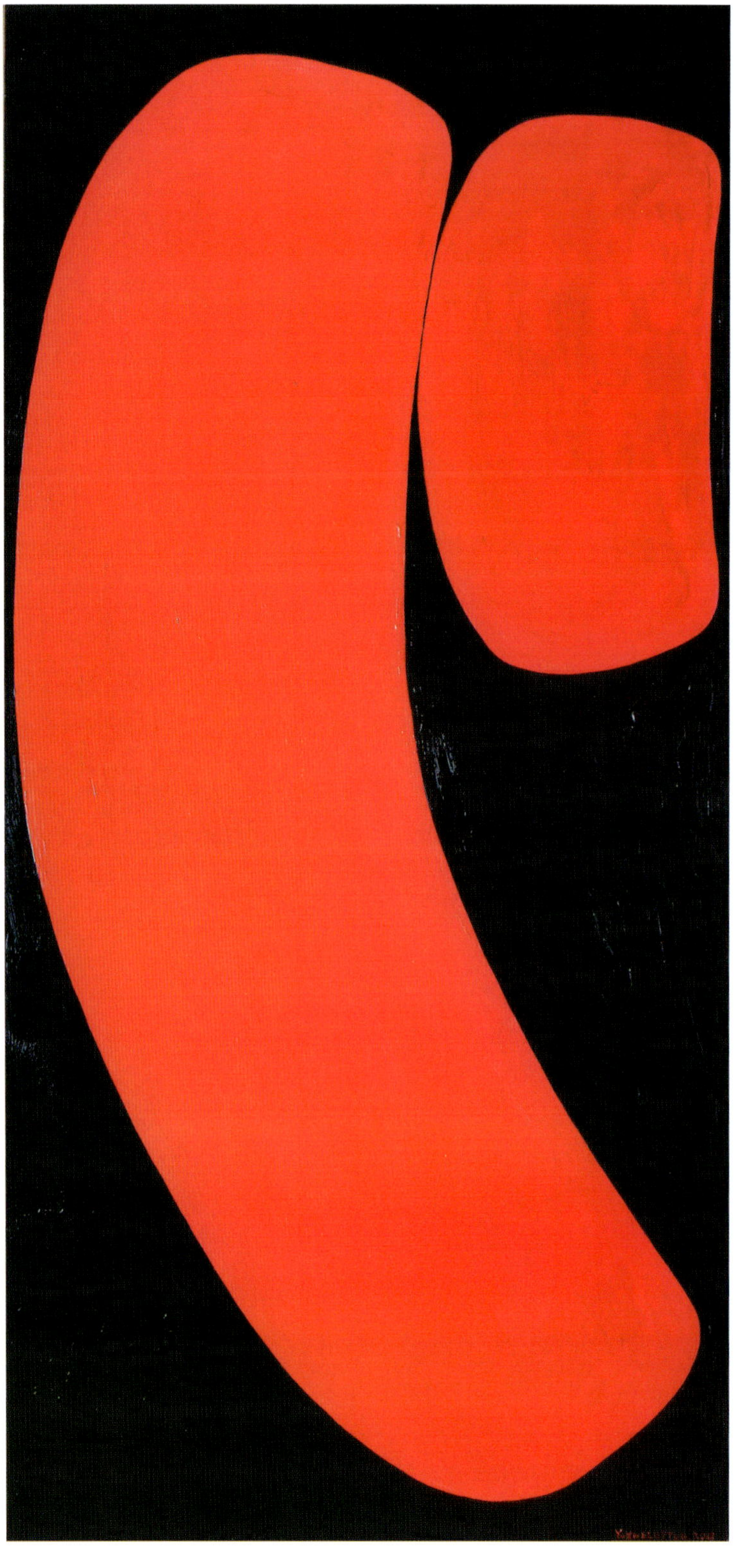

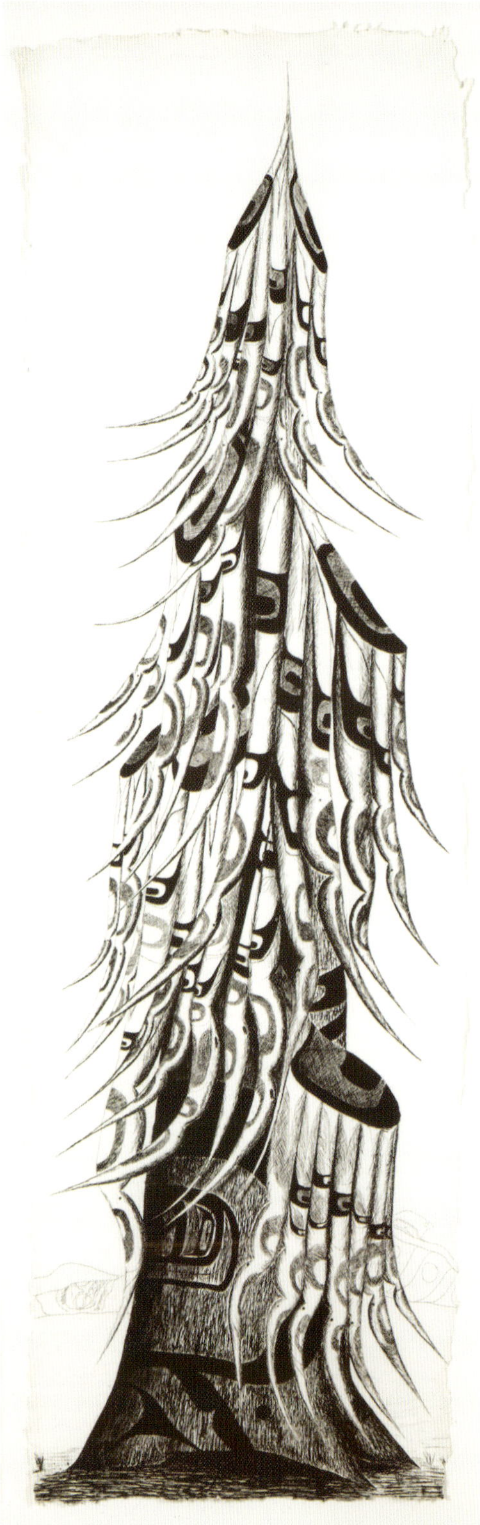

(Left) *Pole Raising,* 2013. Acrylic on canvas. (Right) *The Last Old Growth Spirit Tree*, 2012. Etching on St. Armand paper, edition 7/25.

Yuxweluptun began his ovoid work in the mid-1990s, and what he achieved was combining and creating a Native "modernist" aesthetic by marrying the ancient indigenous Northwest Coast ovoid with high modernist western painterly history. He has commented that during the abstract expressionism and modernist painting periods, Natives were too busy being oppressed and trying to survive for their communities to be part of that particular art movement. In the painting *Ya Right Homie New Transformation Beep Beep Beep the Formline LOL*, eight ovoids all fall within each other, with the exception of a tiny white ovoid in the lower right-hand corner. Using the traditional red, black, and white, the ovoids, stripped of other classic Northwest Coast formline design and coupled with the title, suggest the transformation of the old formline into the contemporary. When his work was first exposed to the public in the early 1980s, there was concern he was either demeaning or changing the traditions of Northwest Coast art. The work *Ya Right Homie New Transformation Beep Beep Beep the Formline LOL* would mess with ancient traditions, and as with all contemporary art, tradition is not fixed, but fluid. Just so, indigenous cultures are not fixed, but transform, adapt, carry forward.

Another large ovoid painting titled *Black Ovoids in Deep Blue Sea* seems murky, even moody. The ocean and its inhabitants are reflected here, as well as how the indigenous ovoid is part of the ocean. The ovoid has now become black, colorless, and surrounded by blue. Considering the many blue periods in western art history, how is one to read this painting? The Indian blues might reflect the fact that many indigenous people are still in survival mode, despite all our accomplishments. As a recent work by another Northwest Coast artist, Skeena Reece, regarding reconciliation and the reality that Canada is finishing its truth and reconciliation commission is titled *I Can Forgive You, But I Am Still Fucked Up* (2013).[8] The United States has yet to officially apologize for the government's and churches' abuses of American Indian people, as Australia and Canada have. These are not just black shapes on blue; as within all Yuxweluptun's work, there are deep sociopolitical undercurrents.

The large canvas titled *Pole Raising*, which references totem pole raising, is a play on words, as the elongated red ovoid points down like a non-erect penis, and the small red ovoid placed neatly underneath is suggestive of male anatomy. This work represents aboriginal masculinity. The verticality of the normally erect pole is now flaccid as a result and symbol of the criminalization of Northwest Coast culture. Due to that criminalization, totem pole making and raising was dormant for many years. In many communities, celebrations of pole raising have not been seen for decades. In some communities, they have not raised any new poles for centuries. *Pole Raising* encompasses the complexity of criminalizing culture and the spiritual harm that are the casualties of cultural imperialism. It further illustrates how indigenous male masculinity and sexuality have been displaced as a result of sexual abuse in the residential schools in Canada and the United States, as well as how white male patriarchy disavowed indigenous male authority.

The painting *Caution! You Are Entering a Free State of Mind Zone* is one of his first ovoid works in this scale. The colorful ovoids are flying across a dark blue background, indicating mobility and freedom, seemingly representing the immensity of the universe of indigenous freedom.

The Direction of Land Claim Negotiations is painted with the traditional red, white, and black. The black background with a large white ovoid dominates the space. Inside the white ovoid is a smaller black ovoid with an even smaller red ovoid nestled in but turned to the opposite direction. Another small red ovoid floats in the upper left-hand corner, and another larger, deeper red ovoid overlaps the pile of white, black, and red ovoids that are all floating. In the lower right-hand corner, a flattened, narrower white ovoid almost touches the pile. The scene is not chaotic, but there is a disconnect between the red and white ovoids. As with most of his titles, viewers are given insight into Yuxweluptun's intentions. In this case, *The Direction of Land Claim Negotiations* indicates that there is not fluidity to the directions, but rather the opposite. The ovoids are piled on each other and face opposite directions, thus indicating that land claims and the finality of negotiations do not meet and common ground simply does not exist, perhaps because goodwill on behalf of the state and public is lacking. The complex reality of modern-day treaty-making in Canada, and especially on the west coast, is that real treaty-making negotiations are going on even 160 years after contact. The ovoids appear to be directionless, indicating that treaty talks are going nowhere, fast.

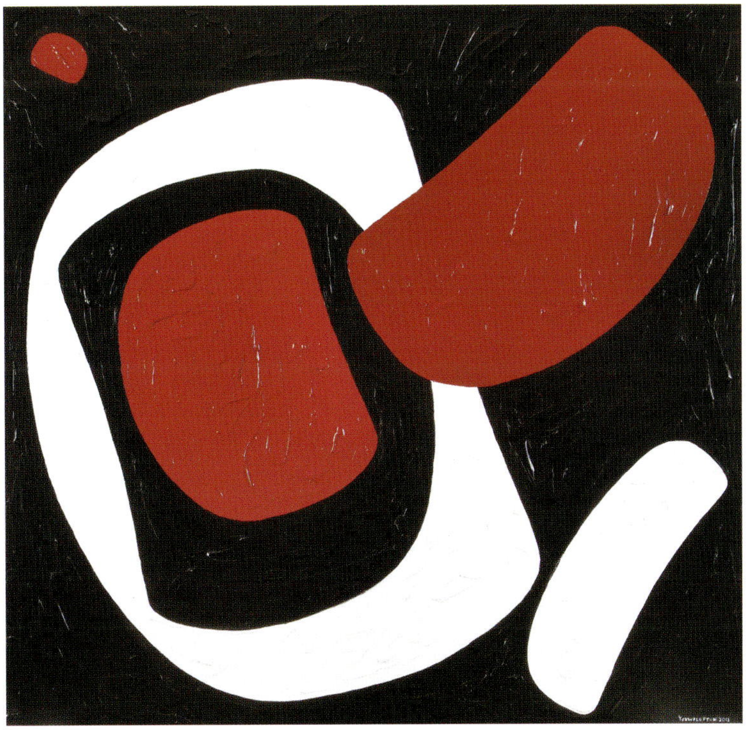

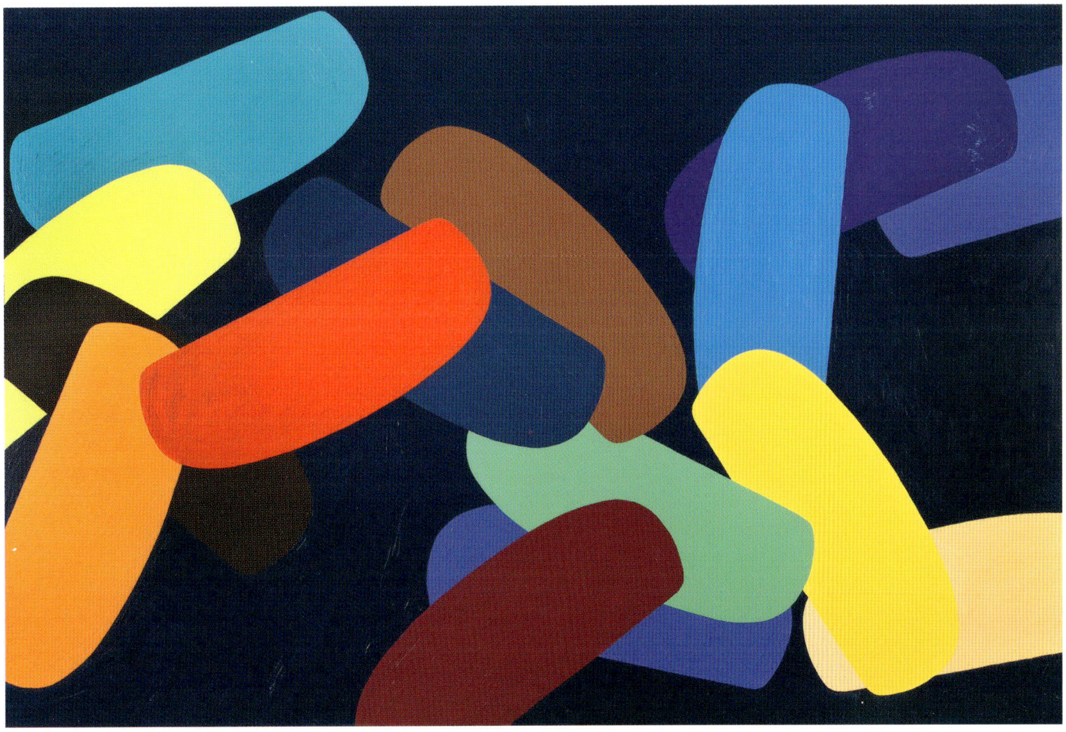

(Above) *The Direction of Land Claim Negotiations*, 2013. Acrylic on canvas. (Below) *Caution! You Are Entering a Free State of Mind Zone*, 2000. Acrylic on canvas.

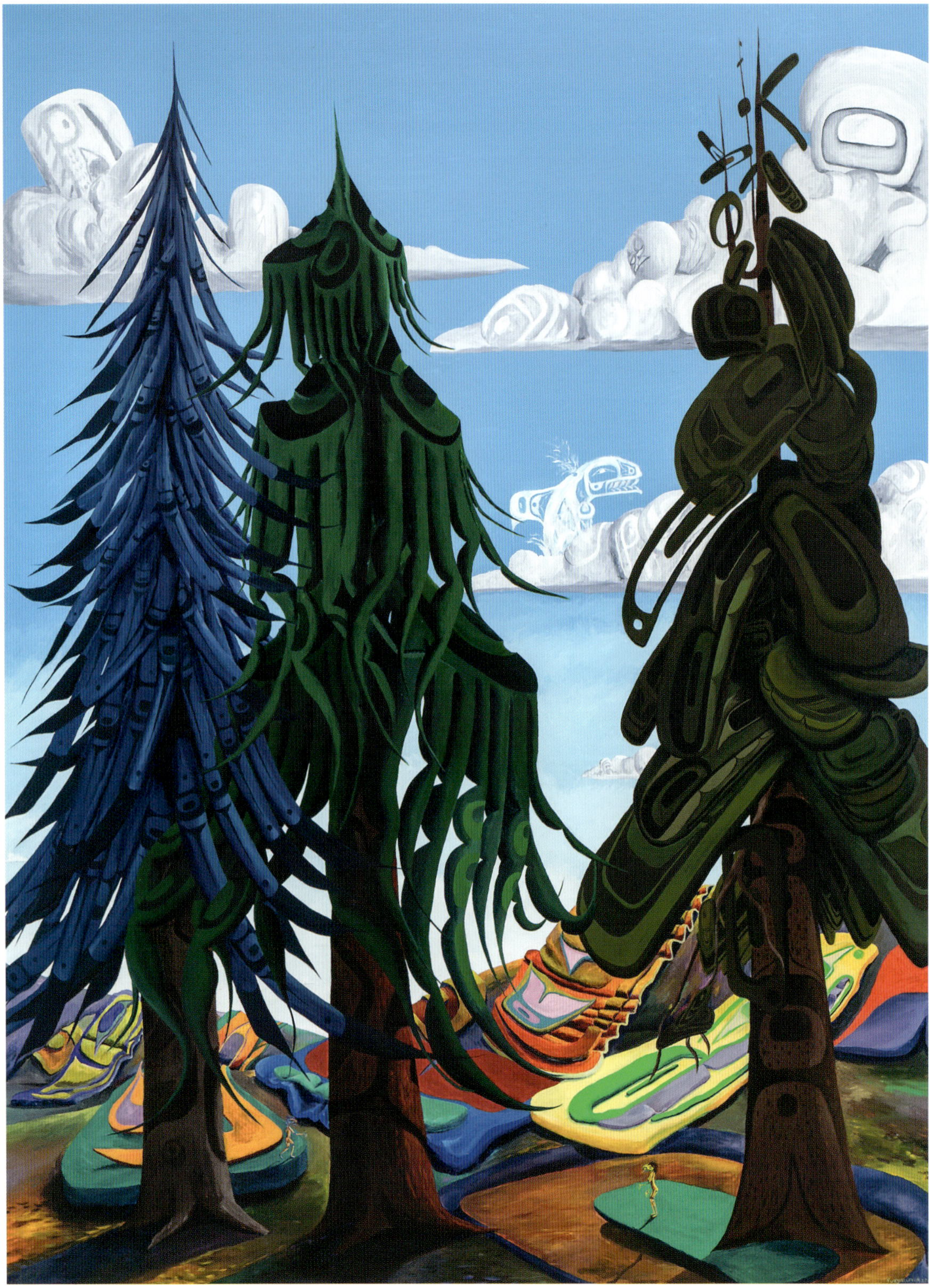

Indian World My Home and Native Land, 2012. Acrylic on canvas. Image courtesy Macaulay & Co. Fine Art. Photo by Barb Choit.

The set of three ink drawings of *White Man Speaks with Forked Tongue, Land Claims Consultant I-III* features male figures, looking slyly in profile, all dressed in suits and ties. Their long tongues extend from their mouths, and all speak with forked tongues. They are rendered as a cross between snake and fox, with large pig snouts. One has a dog-like face. These drawings are similar to his large-scale paintings in which he has rendered Indian agents, consultants, land claims lawyers, and corporate men as a cast of bandits and thieves.

In the painting *Fucking Creeps They're Environmental Terrorists*, three mutated human figures represent corporate oil greed. The men in suits are literally standing thigh-high in oil, and two have forked tongues flailing from their mouths and oil dripping down their chins. It is as though the gluttony for oil extraction is oozing out of their bodies and dripping back down onto the old spill right next to the crying, oil-soaked duck. Yuxweluptun has stated:

> *They are oil executives and criminals at the same time, British Petroleum, the tar sands, and Shell. The Shell guy with the pump in his hand is a real prick and as Shell says, "We pump for you." This is another history painting of the rules of the rich and how they rule the planet and don't have to listen to my Indian voice. That's what happens when you have a republic—they run the planet, blissfully, romantically, pure colonial power. This painting is their dream, their reality, they are happy in their element. They love power that destroys and makes money. They have standing armies and they don't answer to anyone.*[9]

Indian World My Home and Native Land is a classic Yuxweluptun landscape painting. The trees are alive with branches that look like arms with wispy fingers and hands, and the land has eyes and mouths. The three trees are green, blue, and brownish blue. Each is painted in a different style; they all look like the ancients, the grand cedars in Yuxweluptun's traditional territory of Vancouver. The land in the background demonstrates his vivid palette. He is a painter's painter, and a "master mixer" of paint. He likes creating different palettes for different paintings, and he does not want to be just a high contrast painter. He has stated that some painters get caught in the same palette for years. Yuxweluptun is looking for and challenging modern paint and constantly testing color theory. As he tries to set a mood and a color experience for each painting, he wants the viewer to enjoy the palettes. Each painting is a color challenge for him. As far as natural color theory goes, he works from instinct. He walks up to a canvas and sometimes the color is there, and at other times, there is a challenge. He begins to mix.

Well, it's in your mixing, when you want paint to sit side by side, you mix a touch, a value structure that you may want—half of your painting is resolved by what daylight you are using, you decide ok...this is a daytime tone, or a nighttime tone, that simplifies everything— whether painting a daytime scene or nighttime scene. When I started the abstract stuff, I was trying to create a palette of ovoidism, at first the surface was hard edged and now I am giving them texture and getting in the material and considering what the brush strokes can really do. That feeling of walking up to a canvas and then you begin, that's a beautiful feeling when I approach a new canvas. Right now, I have fifty different containers of pigments and I take a combo of colors and see how they work. I work with anywhere from six to fourteen different palettes on a given painting. I mix as I go along. Once you make a decision, you have to mix enough paint for the entire painting. I like the challenge of creating new colors.[10]

In the work *Portrait of a Residential School Child*, the image of the child is colorful and hopeful, and he is surrounded by a golden crown/glow like that of a saint. Yuxweluptun went to the Kamloops Indian Residential

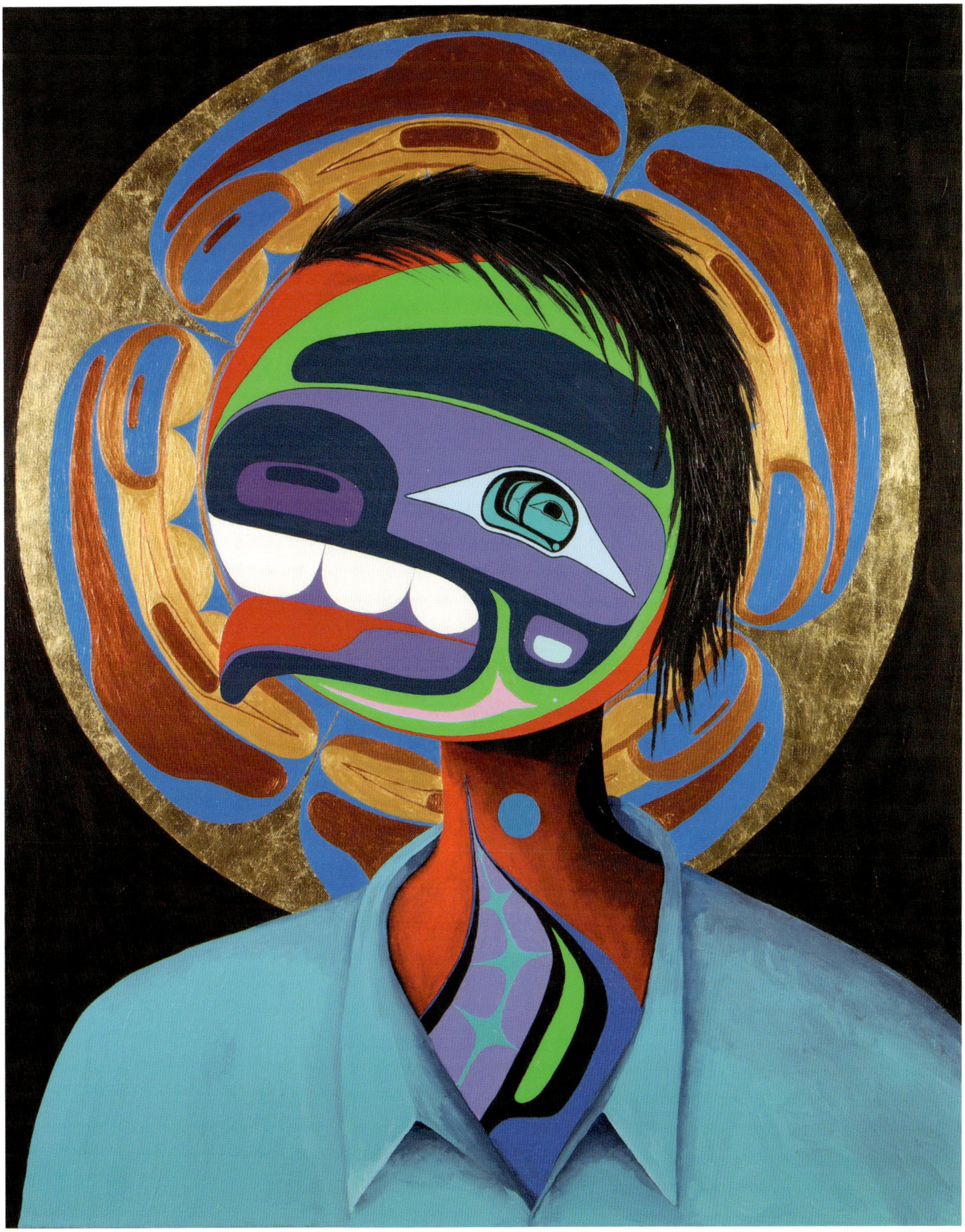

Portrait of a Residential School Child, 2005. Acrylic on canvas.

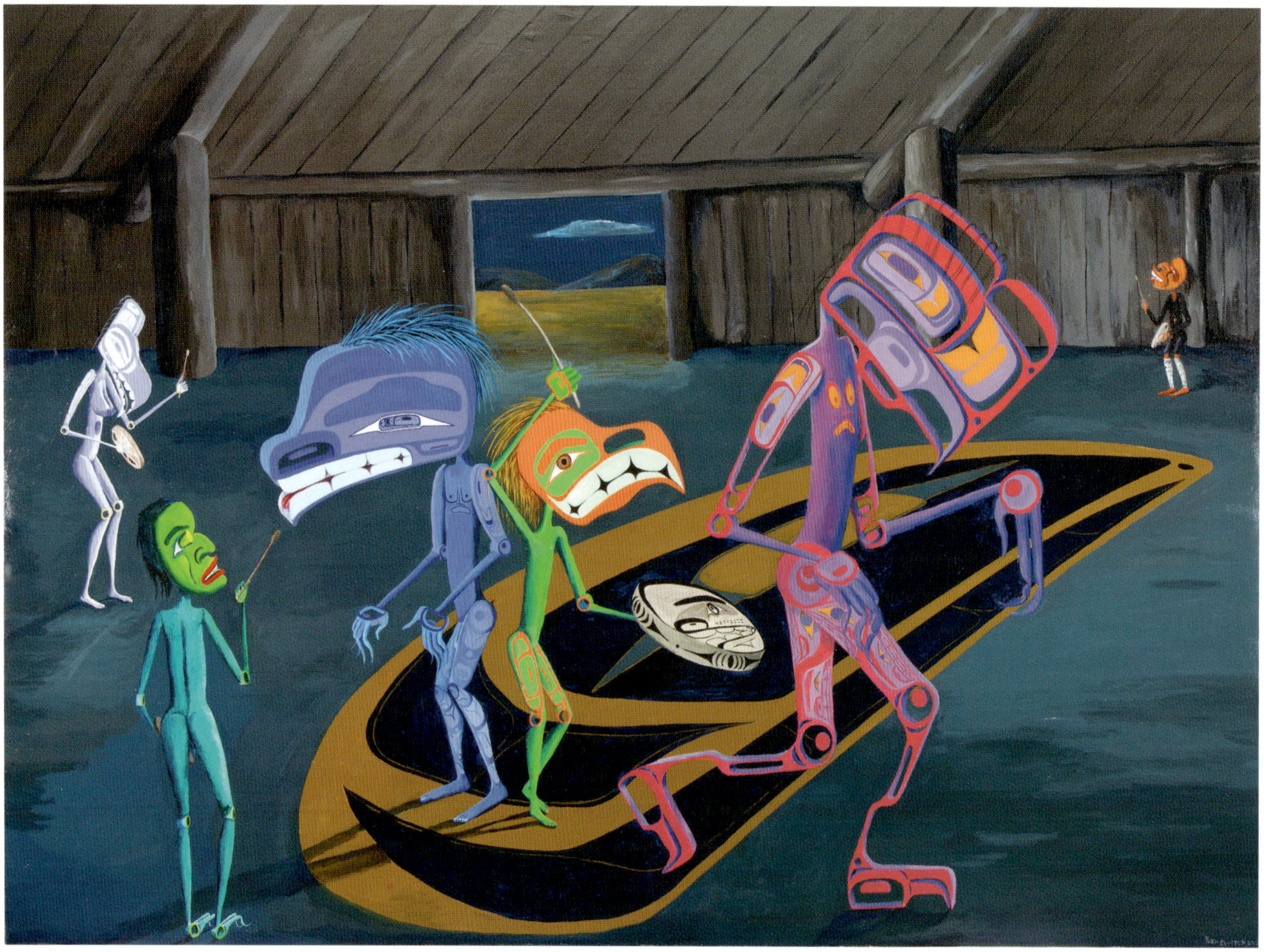

Floor Opener, 2013. Acrylic on canvas.

School before "the law was changed," and while there, he went to a funeral for a girl from his class who died from an apparent wood tick bite. Indians kids were buried outside, beside "playgrounds"; they were not sent back home to their families. In Canada, research is still determining how many children "died," and recently, human biomedical experimentation at some of the schools has been exposed. These schools were also well known for harboring clergy pedophiles, which has left a deep scar on healthy indigenous sexuality. It is a grim part of the Native American/First Nations (Canadian) experience, and to not discuss it would be an act of denial, erasure, even cowardice. Yuxweluptun has turned his residential school child into a saint; the boy wears a turquoise shirt, the color of healing. His skin is red, his hair is brown, but his eye is turquoise and he is surrounded by ancient tribal iconography; this design is also tattooed on his body. This Indian boy has survived.

Floor Opener, the most spiritual narrative of the works, depicts dancers and drummers in the longhouse. Of the six figures in the painting, only one is clothed, which seems to indicate this one is human. The rest of the five beings are of various sizes and colors. Some have see-through body parts, indicating they are spirit beings. The large purplish being in the foreground is on the move, as if circling and preparing the space for human dancers as well as the spirit that has been invoked to join the humans. The door into the longhouse looks out onto the mountains where the spirit of the mountain dwells, and the light ash falling from the ceiling is from the ritual fires that burn all winter. The ash is a being itself. Invoking the spirits and ancestors is done through dance, song, and the drum. Yuxweluptun has painted and drawn the sacred longhouse before and was the first artist to exhibition a virtual reality work of the longhouse in the early 1990s in *Inherent Rights, Vision Rights*. Of all the Northwest Coast tribes, the Salish have rarely let researchers into their longhouses and do not sell their dance masks at market, and by doing so, they have maintained a significant connection to other realms.

In the year 2013, Yuxweluptun paints and makes contemporary art in his 5,000-square-foot studio on his familial ancient homeland. His hereditary name is Yuxweluptun, which means "Man of Many Masks." These masks are held in families by the women and danced by the men. He is a spirit dancer, a black face dancer, and has danced his families' masks. The mountains of the north shore and the spirit of the mountains comfort him, as does the Salish Sea. He lives where his ancestors have walked, danced, hunted, and fished for thousands of years. The soul of this place called Vancouver is wrapped up with the masks of the Salish people—his ancestors and contemporary living family. He was recently given another name, Let'lo:ts'teltun—"Man of Many Colors." And as he mixes his fifty containers of paint, he is asking us, the viewers of his art, to respect and acknowledge that lineage and to acknowledge and respect earth. All my relations. Everything is related. *Mitakuye Oyasin.*[11]

---

[1]Lawrence Paul Yuxweluptun, interview with author, July 15, 2013.

[2]Ibid.

[3]The author notes that this is a common phrase that Yuxweluptun uses in his lectures and presentations.

[4]"Chief Sitting Bull," accessed August 1, 2013, http://www.indigenouspeople.net/sittbull.htm.

[5]The author is suggesting that painting in general is a primitive act, and she has attempted to remove the value judgment associated with the word "primitive" by declaring that all cultures have an indigenous past, and have rendered their existence via marking on surfaces.

[6]Victor Masayesva, *Indigenous Experimentalism, Magnetic North* (Minneapolis, MN: Minnesota University Press, Walker Art Centre, and Video Pool Inc., 2000), 228–239.

[7] W. Jackson Rushing III, *Native American Art and the New York Avant-Garde: A History of Cultural Primitivism* (Austin, TX: University of Texas Press, 1995).

[8]The Helen and Morris Belkin Gallery at the University of British Columbia recently commissioned Skeena Reece to make this single channel video installation for the group show *Witnesses: Art and Canada's Indian Residential Schools.*

[9]Lawrence Paul Yuxweluptun, interview with author, July 25, 2013.

[10]Ibid.

[11]*Mitakuye Oyasin* is Lakota for "All my relations."

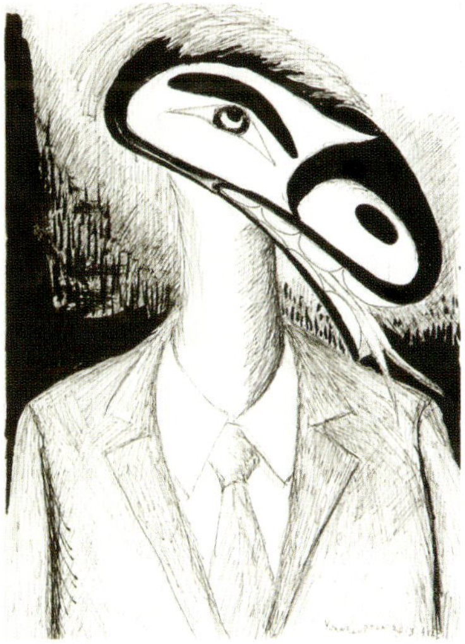

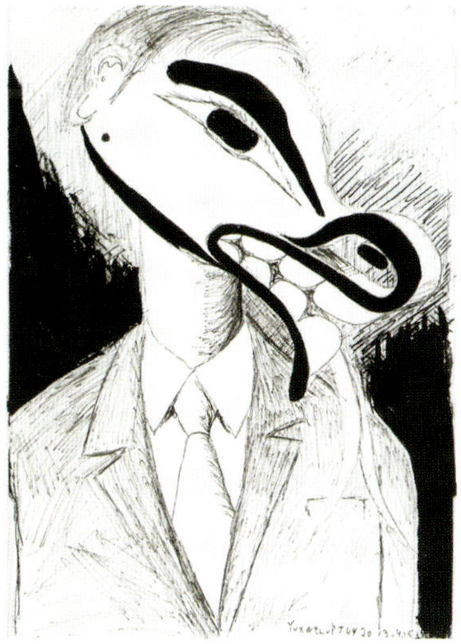

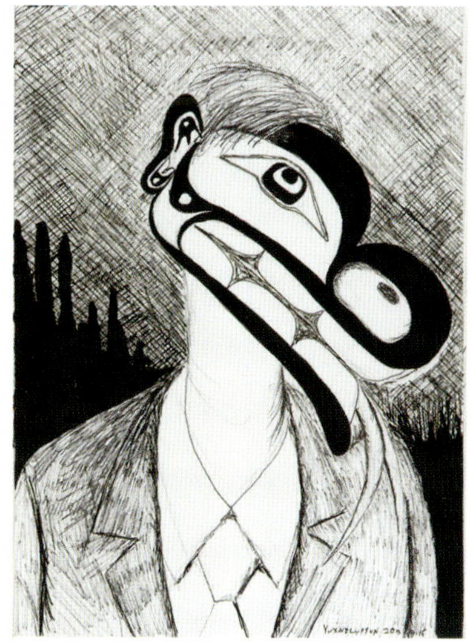

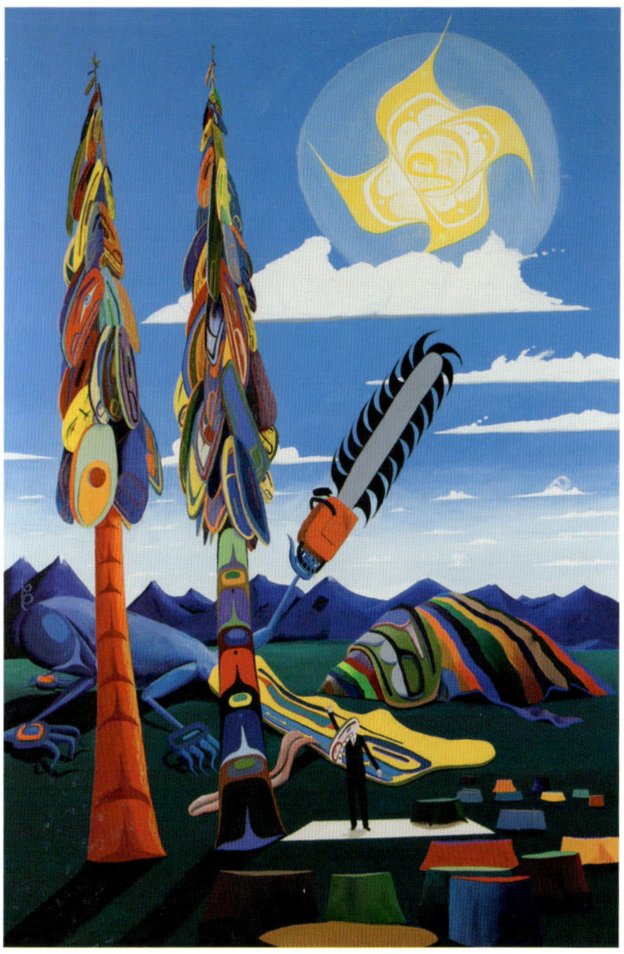

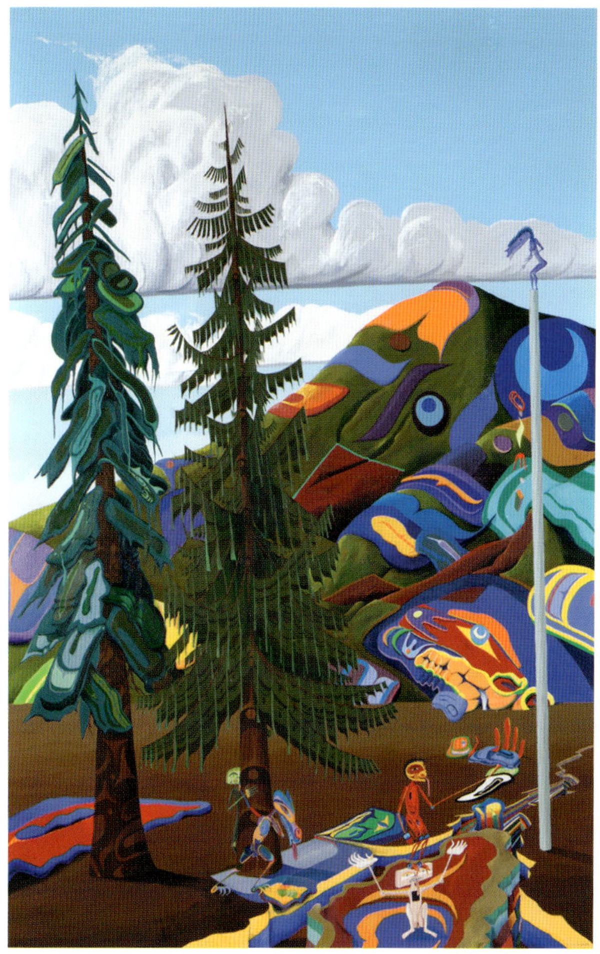

(Above) *White Man Speaks with Forked Tongue, Land Claims Consultant I, II,* and *III*, 2013. Pen on paper. (Below left) *The New Legend: The Screaming Liberal, Begging for a Referendum on Land Claims*, 1999. Acrylic on canvas. (Below right) *Losing Identities*, 1999. Acrylic on canvas.

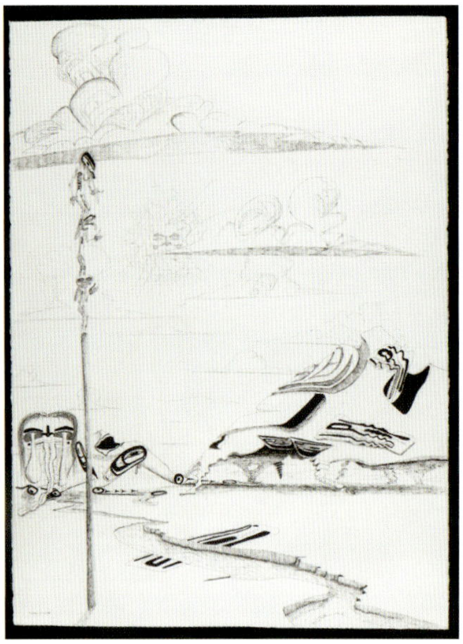

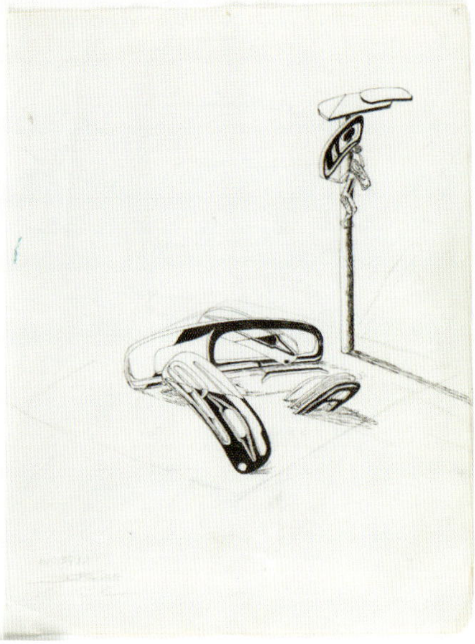

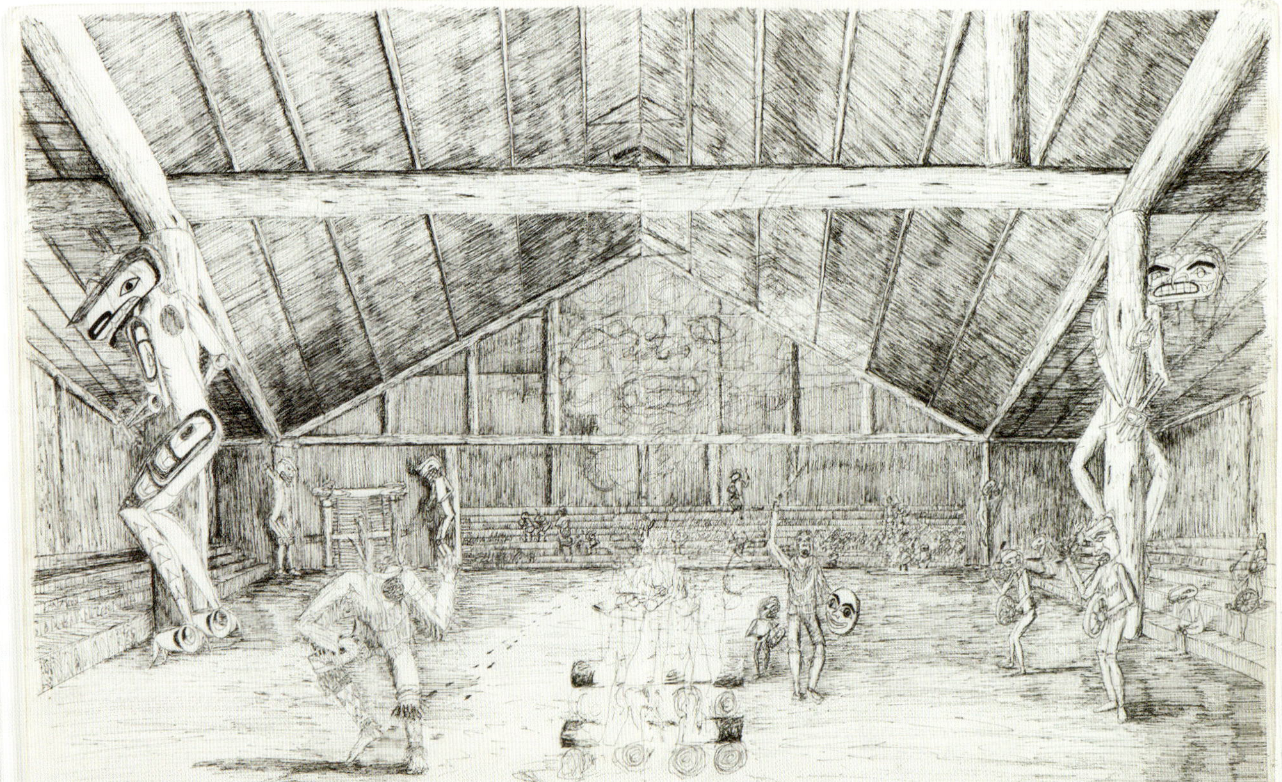

(Above left) *One Night in the Forest,* 1994. Pen on paper. (Above right) *Untitled (Landscape)*, 1987. Pen on paper. (Below) *Untitled* (Longhouse Interior), date unknown. Pen and pencil on paper.

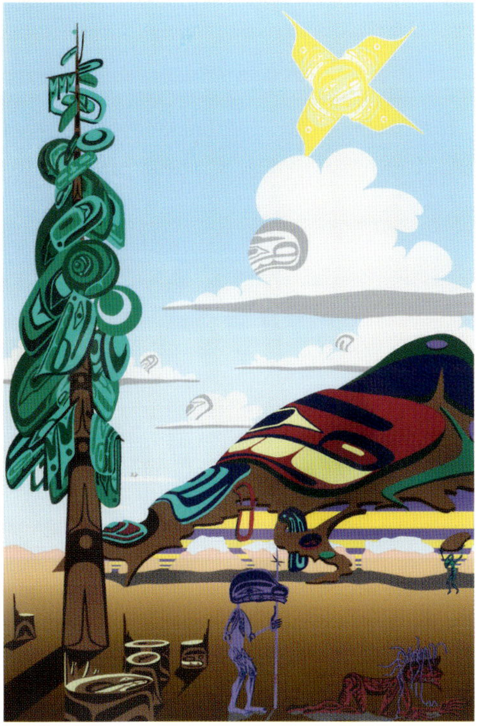

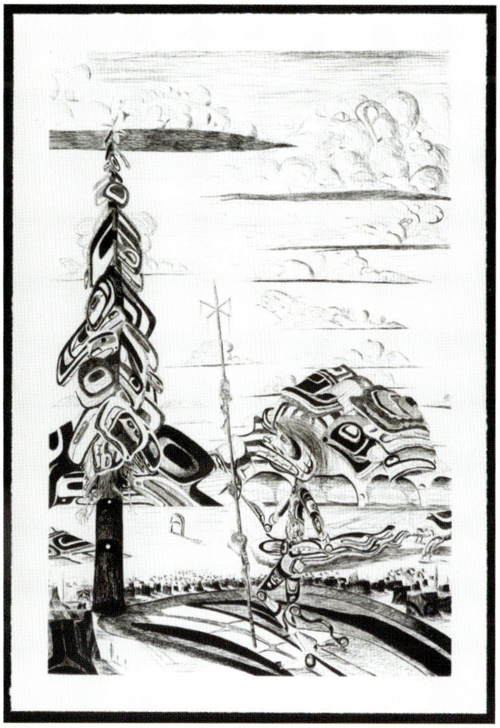

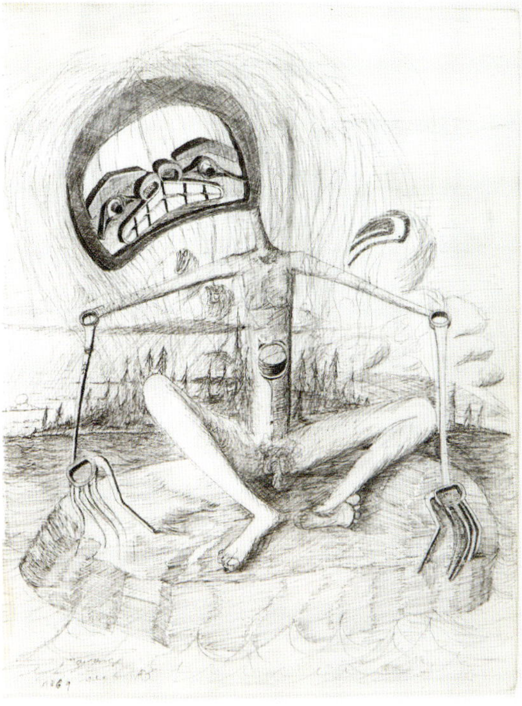

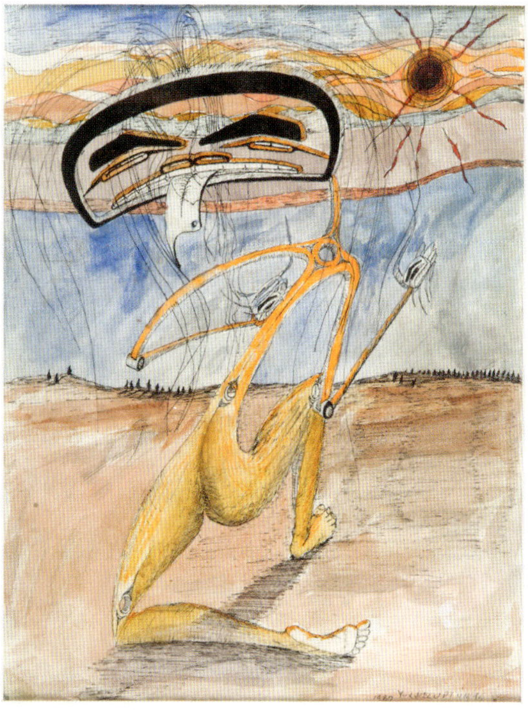

(Above left) *Clear Cut to the Last Tree*, 1993. Screenprint, edition 6/98. (Above right) *Super Clear Cut*, 1993. Etching, edition 5/90. (Below left) *Untitled* (Figure), 1985. Pen and pencil on paper. (Below right) *Untitled (Figure)*, 1980-1995. Pen and watercolor on paper.

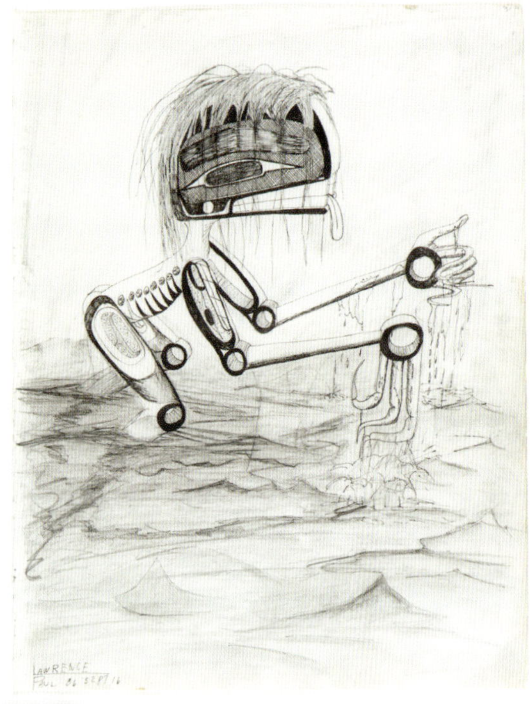

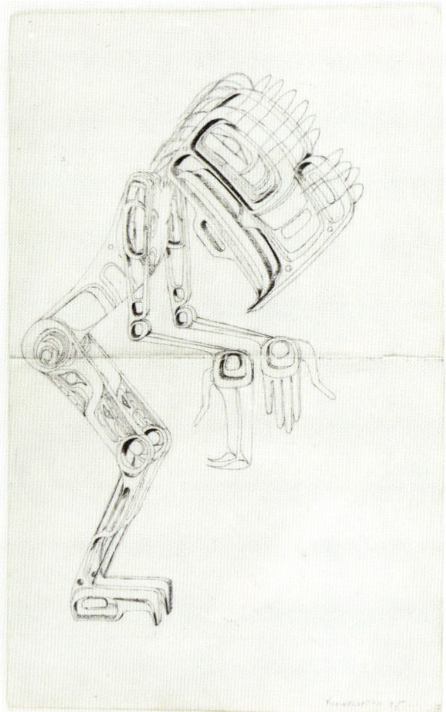

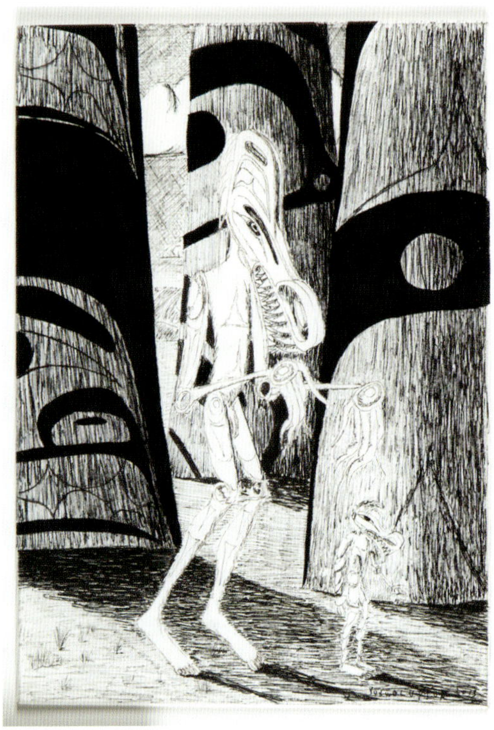

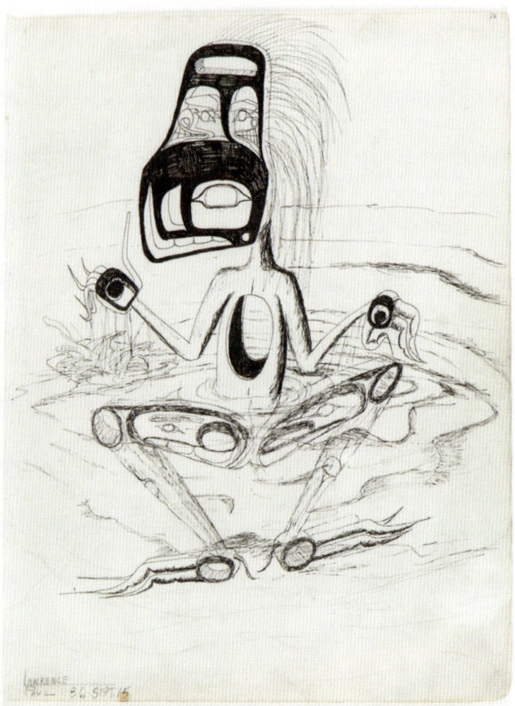

(Above left) *Untitled*, 2013. Pen on paper. (Above right) *Untitled*, 1986. Pen and pencil on paper. (Below left) *Untitled*, 1986. Pen and pencil on paper. (Below right) *Untitled (Figure)*, 1995. Pen and ink on paper.

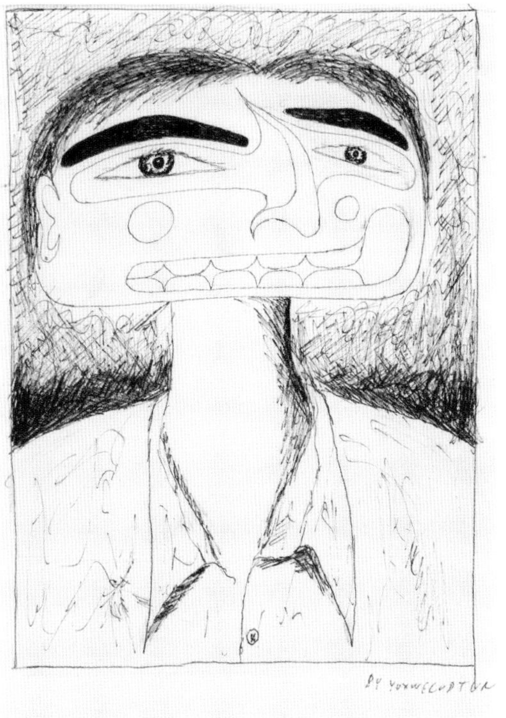

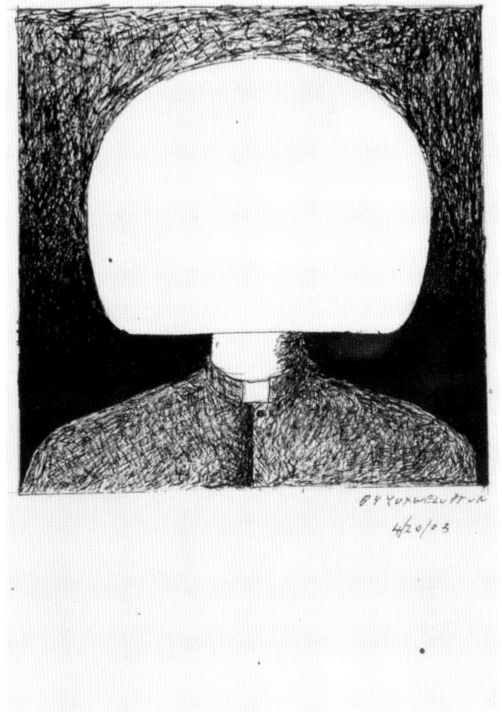

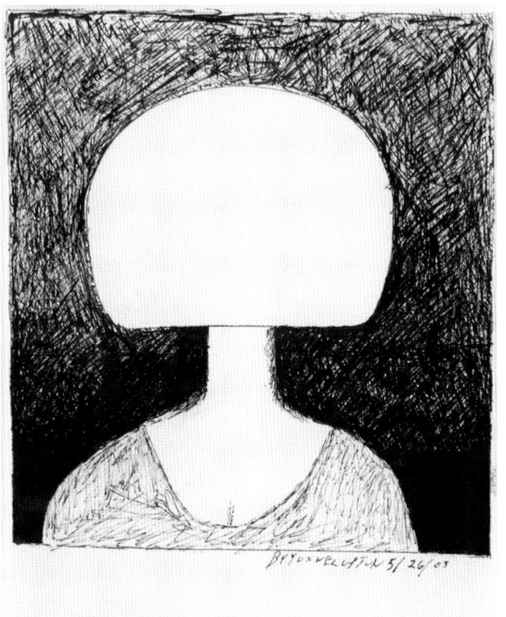

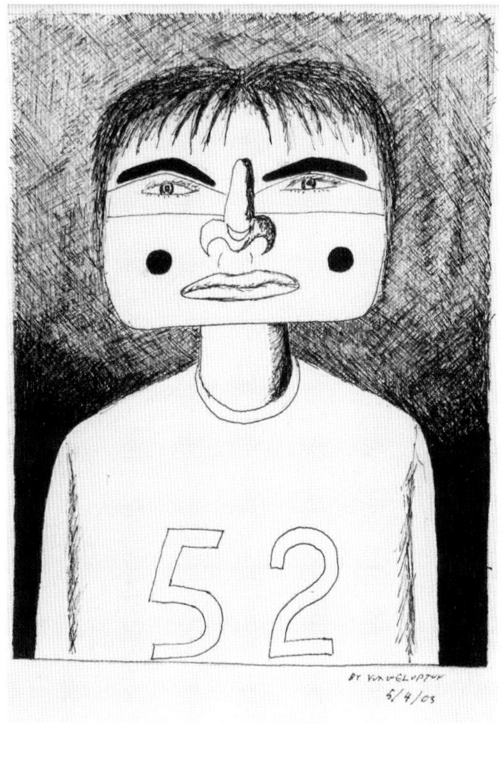

(Above left) *Untitled Portrait*, 2003. Pen on paper. (Above right) *Untitled Portrait*, 2003. Pen on paper. (Below left) *Untitled Portrait*, 2003. Pen on paper. (Below right) *Untitled Portrait*, 2003. Pen on paper.

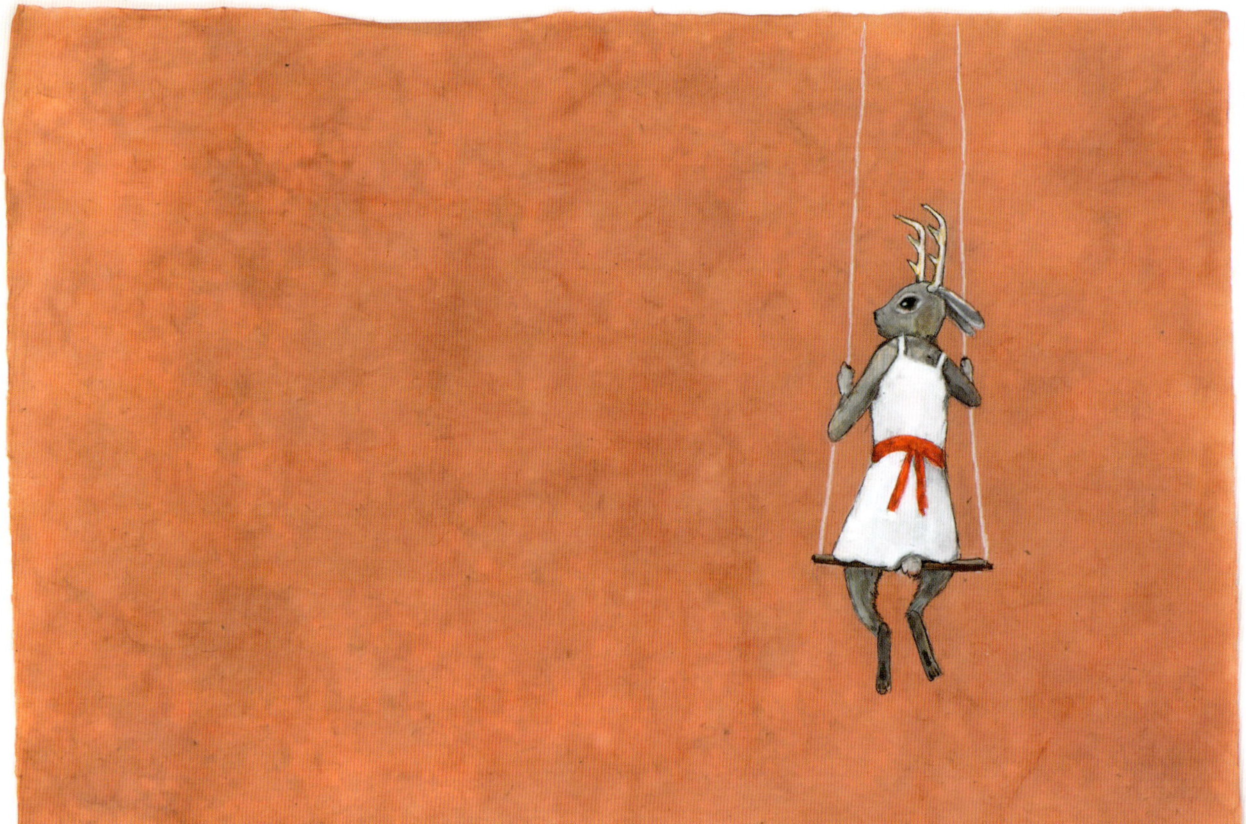

Fearsome Critter, 2012. Mixed media on paper. Image courtesy the Bockley Gallery.

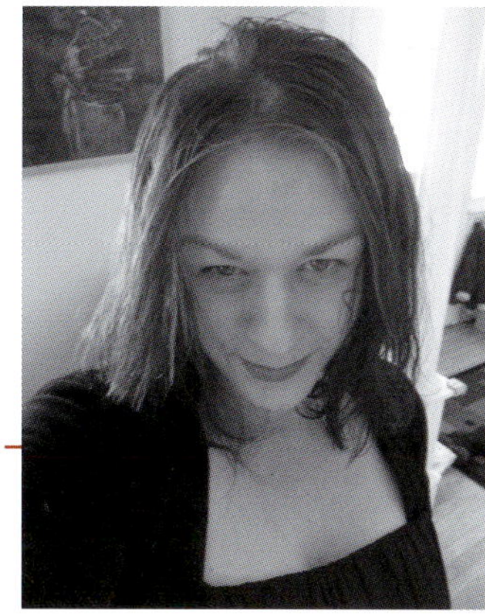

Julie Buffalohead

(Ponca Tribe of Oklahoma)

Fighter of the Good Fight

Jennifer Complo McNutt

My recent series reflects a journey of a more personal nature. The narrative tension my work creates emanates from the Native oral tradition of storytelling, while I blend in my own distinct strands of make-believe.

Julie Buffalohead dreams a world. It is a world where oppressive societal mores are reenacted, challenged, and overcome by the meek. Small animals, rabbits and raccoons, birds and bears, and even Coyote the trickster have moments of tenderness, despair, and triumph as they meander through the ambiguous spaces of Buffalohead's paintings.

The fine, facile drawings are accentuated with the modeled and measured application of paint. It is an application that creates a quiet understanding of each element it describes, be it architectural or animal. Buffalohead creates a theater in the settings of her paintings: the woods, the bathroom, and the front yard, in a sandbox or a wading pool. The understated settings are the stage for monsters of domesticity, myths of motherhood, a fairytale history of America, personal experiences, and homage to Ponca culture. All are expressed through Buffalohead's private visual language, a language so intriguing that it transports the viewer to another worldview: hers.

Born in 1972, Buffalohead is an enrolled member of the Ponca Tribe of Oklahoma. She received her bachelor of fine arts degree from the Minneapolis College of Art and Design in 1995 and a master of fine arts degree from Cornell University in 2001. She currently resides in Minneapolis and has received many prestigious awards, including the McKnight

Foundation Fellowship for Visual Arts and a Jerome Foundation Travel and Study Grant. A prolific artist, Buffalohead pursues in her current work a tireless personal and sociopolitical investigation based on being a woman, mother, Native, and conscientious observer.

Kay WalkingStick, Buffalohead's art professor at Cornell University, gives insight into the place where the artist started her educational and artistic journey.

Julie and I were at Cornell together. I was the professor and she the student and our relationship was certainly instructive for me. I hope it was for Julie, too. She came to Cornell with some very solid ideas about herself in the art world and how she should be making art. Those are useful qualities for a graduate student in the fine arts. She drew animals with alacrity and seemed to have a real affinity & and respect for them.

Buffalohead challenges commonly held conventions of societal mores. One physical manifestation of that challenge is her disregard for traditionally based compositions, replaced by an unconventional use that often creates a feeling of being out of balance. This manipulation of compositions illuminates the roles each character has to perform. Fine lines and fragile geometry that define rabbit's staffs or the ropes of a swing with groupings slightly heavy in one quadrant of the paper give compositional cues about the tenacious yet delicate balance Buffalohead creates in her world.

In each painting, the drama unfolds subtly with quiet tension, perhaps starting with amusement at the rabbit or doll house. This begins the contemplation of the anthropomorphized creature and the revelation of the intensity of the scene and its sense of foreboding. The foreshadowing of a tragedy finally leads back to amusement at the clever and cunning use of children, animals, and playthings to act out the dissolution, confusion, misrepresentations, and pain that are familiar and undesirable to us all.

Buffalohead's pregnancy marked the beginning of her foray into the use of paper and the investigation of negative space in a new way. She isolates the scene centrally in the color field of handmade paper.

I use an artisan paper called Lokta, handmade in Nepal, pounded from the bark of a shrub—which I feel is an artistic object in itself. The paper, which I started working with about five years ago, transformed my work, where I had less of an emphasis on filling negative space with a background—but instead, using the negative space in relation to the figures.[1]

Buffalohead suspends reality in her painted scenes that appear random, like automatic drawing, but which are presented as automatic storytelling. She compiles images from animal and human cultures in likely and unlikely situations, doing what is necessary to wade through the moment.

When I work on a drawing, I take vellum and draw out my figures. Then I cut them out and arrange them on the surface. When I am satisfied with the arrangement I redraw the figures onto the paper. Many of my decisions on how a drawing will evolve are based on this initial preparation. I sometimes will draw two figures to establish a relationship and add objects on the basis of a composition I achieved with the cut-outs. The narrative is sort of "spun up" in this way, during this design phase, where there is a very active dialogue between the participants, the figures, or animals. This is a creative phase where sometimes there are a lot of evolutions and different ideas.[2]

Before the birth of her daughter, Buffalohead revisited her own childhood and examined the societal expectations of little girls in the *Tea Party* series, which distills symbols of femininity. As with many of Buffalohead's titles, the tea party refers to societal expectations. The myths of an idyllic childhood and even motherhood often seem at best foreign to Buffalohead and at worst a hopelessly uncompromising gender role meant to govern behavior and appearance.

In "Tea Party Day One," I was revisiting childhood with a young girl having a tea party with coyotes and other animals. Wearing a mask, she feeds her stuffed bear. Her world is interrupted by the trickster coyote, also in a mask. The role play of dressing up, wearing lipstick, nurturing dolls, and feeding teddy bears reinforces societies' expectations of little girls. The stereotypical feminine roles of wife and mother are assigned to girls and [influence] their choice of toys and games.[3]

As things progress in the *Tea Party* series, "the animals have taken over. Now they are participating in the little girl's rituals. They mock the human world."[4] In *Tea Party Day One*, Coyote interrupts this world that, even if it is a façade, is the girl's current reality. The trickster appears, and by *Tea Party Day Three*, the animals have taken over. The fantasy disappears, as does the little girl. The idea of mocking or being mocked that is introduced in the *Tea Party* series is a recurring theme throughout Buffalohead's work. In her world, in virtually every case, it is the animals that mock the human world.

According to Buffalohead, *The Dog Paddle* is about "animals interacting in a human world."[5] They are adapting to their environment by using their natural instincts such as the coyote positioning his arms into a doggie paddle as if swimming in the air over the water. The rabbit jumps into the pool wearing appropriately sized scuba equipment, no matter that rabbits hate water. Nearby, literally floating in air, a second rabbit is bestowing dual honors on the swimming rabbit and coyote with a coup stick and fairy wand.

The facility of her drawing is almost invisible in its understated delineation of the hock of the rabbit as it lifts itself over the edge of the pool. The coyote is planted as firmly as a biped, his paws in motion but in no danger of tipping forward. As with all wily coyotes, the back-turned ears serve to stabilize and keep him aware of any force that may come up from behind to knock him down from this unnatural stance. The second rabbit seemingly floats, inferring the geometry and complexity of the composition—composition that is stable, deliberate, and understated.

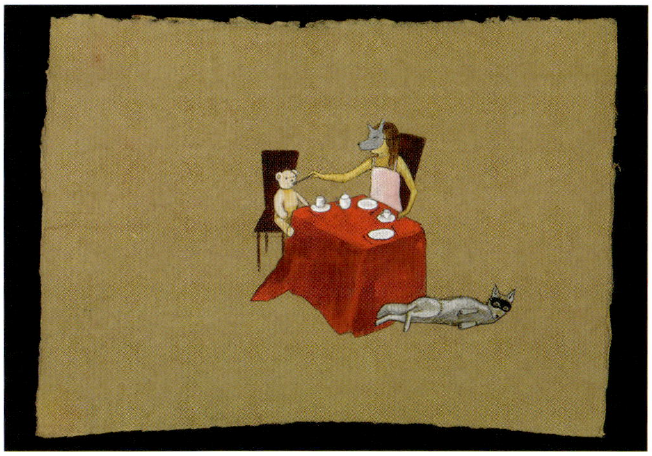

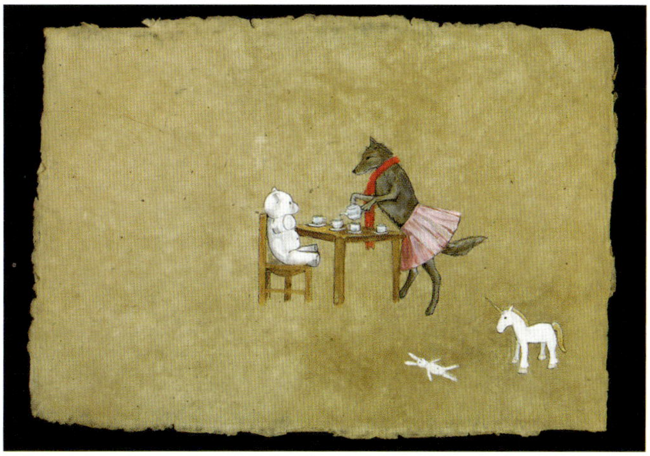

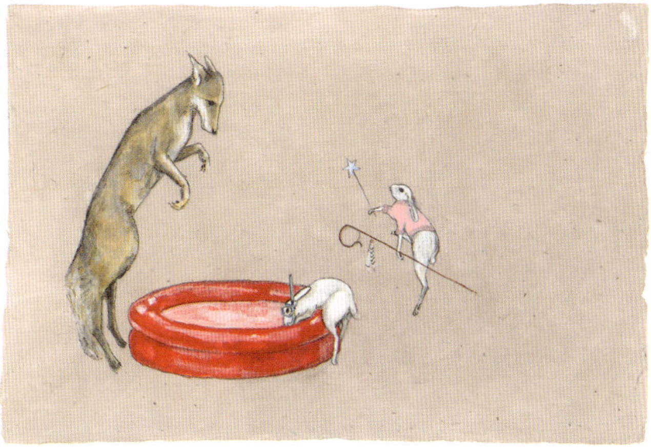

(Tp[) *Tea Party Day One*, 2008. Mixed media on handmade paper. Image courtesy the Bockley Gallery. (Center) *Tea Party Day Three*, 2008. Mixed media on paper. Image courtesy the Bockley Gallery. (Bottom) *The Dog Paddle*, 2012. Mixed media on paper. Image courtesy the Bockley Gallery.

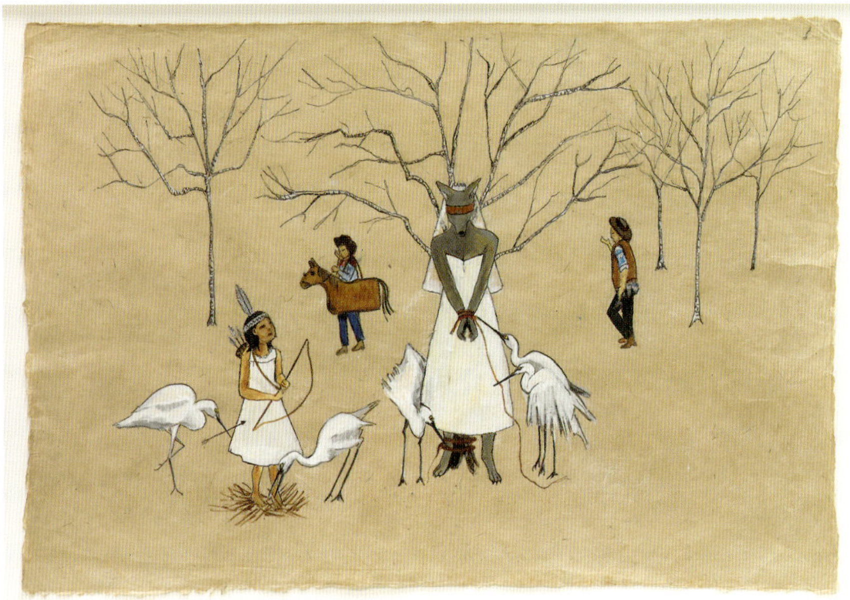

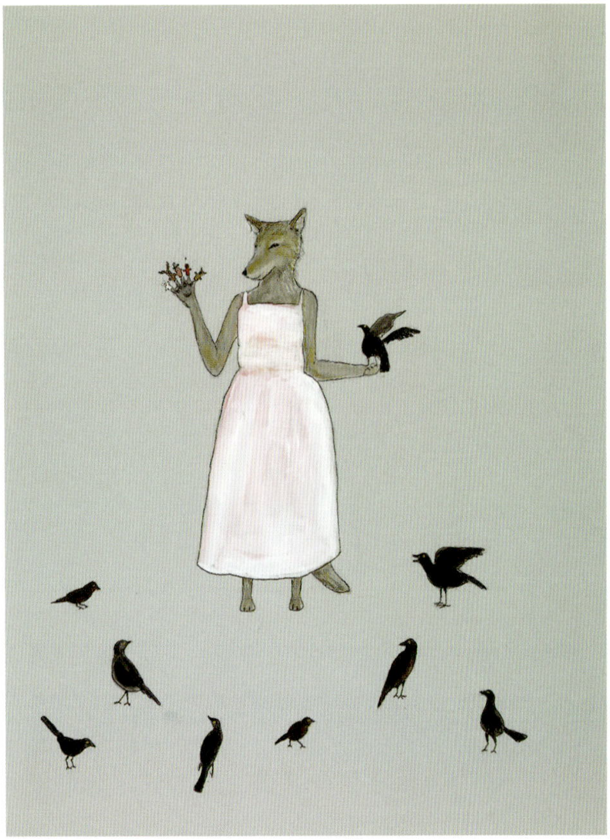

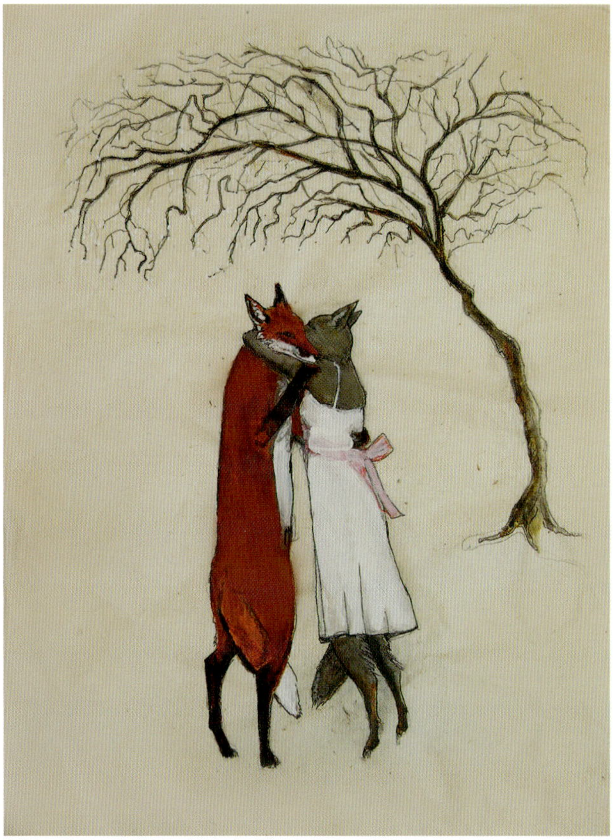

(Above) *The Confirmation*, 2009. Mixed media on paper. Image courtesy National Museum of the American Indian, Smithsonian Institution (268613.000). Photo by NMAI Photo Services. (Below left) *Storyteller*, 2008. Mixed media on paper. Image courtesy the artist. (Below right) *Reconcile*, 2011. Mixed media on paper. Image courtesy the artist.

The coyote is standing above the pool, dog paddling in the air, as some dogs do when held over water. One rabbit is about to dive in and another rabbit is holding a coup stick in one hand and a fairy wand in the other. The rabbit anoints the pool with the fairy wand and wins prestige with his coup stick.[6]

Storyteller references Buffalohead's Native traditions with "a coyote dressed up as a woman performing for the crows with finger puppets on her hand. [The] coyote has taken over the role of storyteller."[7] This lovely lithe coyote, dressed simply with a content and calm expression, enacts a puppet theater for happy feathered friends littered across the page and eager for the words their teacher shares. An example of the Native oral tradition, *Storyteller* is providing lessons in an enjoyable way. It is a stark contrast to the lessons of other works such as *You Have to Play Indian to Be Indian* or *Reconcile*. And still, an interesting parallel exists between the Native oral tradition of storytelling and Buffalohead's narrative drawing and paintings. As with any good story, she is passing along the lessons of the past: some hard and disheartening lessons, some playful and hopeful for the future, but lessons all.

Buffalohead's personal fortitude comes in part from the relationship she maintains with her Ponca culture.

Ponca clans trace descent through the male line, children belonging to the clan of their father. I am a member of the Deer clan, or Eats No Deer or Elk. My father and his father were Deer clan members. Long ago, Deer clan members policed the deer hunt. As a Deer clan member today, I avoid eating deer meat and don't handle deerskin or anything made out of deer hide or bones, which is the respect for my clan ancestor. However, when clan members die, we are supposed to wear deerskin moccasins, so in the spirit world, we are recognized as Deer clan members.[8]

In *The Columbus Prophecies*, Buffalohead is serious in her disapproval of the false impression and stereotypes the dominant culture has assigned to the history and traditions of Native people.

This is a piece of revisionist history in the microcosm of the bathroom. A young girl is in an imaginative world where there is a fox and a rabbit using a bow and arrow and a tomahawk to annihilate Columbus's ship floating in the bathtub. It is an alternative history.[9]

Her seriousness on the matter makes her narrative and sense of humor all the more disarming. A small child heralds an army of the strong of spirit and light of foot. Together they punish the offenders, who, contrary to popular convention, are small and unable to protect themselves. Here turnabout is fair play. The offenders are being punished for stealing and assuming for their own something that is not theirs. Manifest destiny symbolized by Columbus is an abomination of the traditions, peoples, and lifestyle of indigenous people of this country. In the confines of the bathroom, it is made right.

In *Fearsome Critter*, Buffalohead refers to the rabbit/deer as a "hybrid" animal. This "cross or mixture" is enigmatic. Is it more rabbit than deer, based on the number of attributes from both, or are the deer antlers so significant as to trump the overt "rabbitness" of the animal? The work may be interpreted as a foreshadowing of her investigations and experiences with being Native American and biracial and notions of identity and self-image.

This enigma is mirrored in her use of space. Is the swing, which hangs on delicate ropes from the boundaries of the paper, allowing the rabbit to propel into the deep space forward happily and rhythmically swinging until eventually she leaps into the infinity of space before her? Or is she up against the wall, stopped? Either way, it appears that what is beneath her is bottomless.

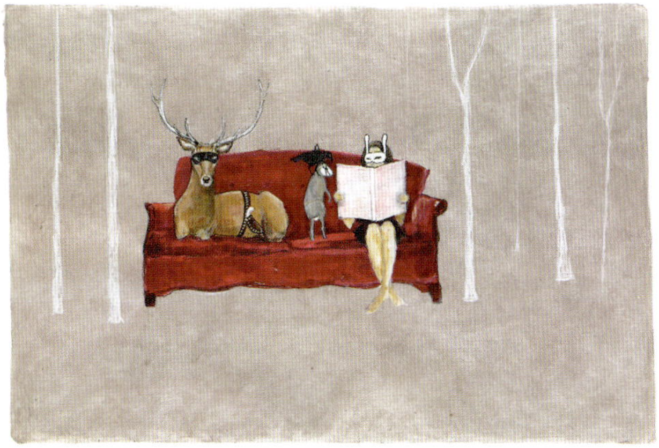

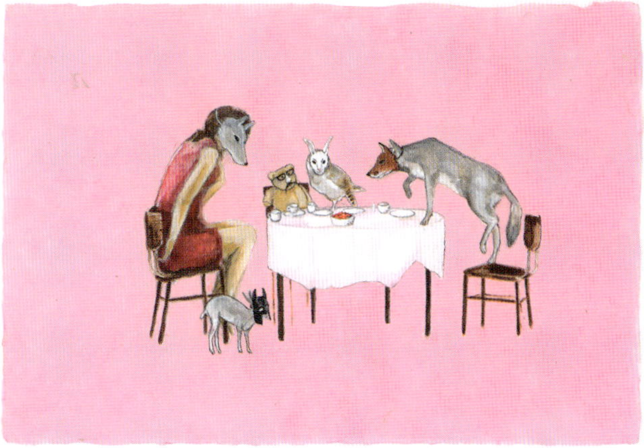

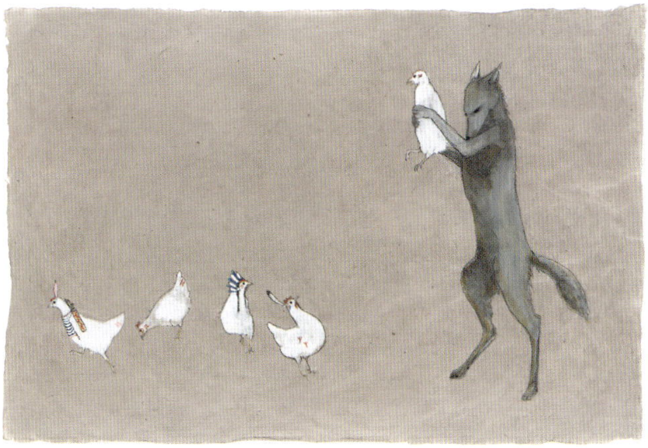

(Top) *The Lone Ranger Rides Again*, 2012. Mixed media on paper. Image courtesy the Bockley Gallery. (Center) *The Standoff,* 2012. Mixed media on paper. Image courtesy the Bockley Gallery. (Bottom) *Warpaint,* 2012. Mixed media on paper. Image courtesy the Bockley Gallery.

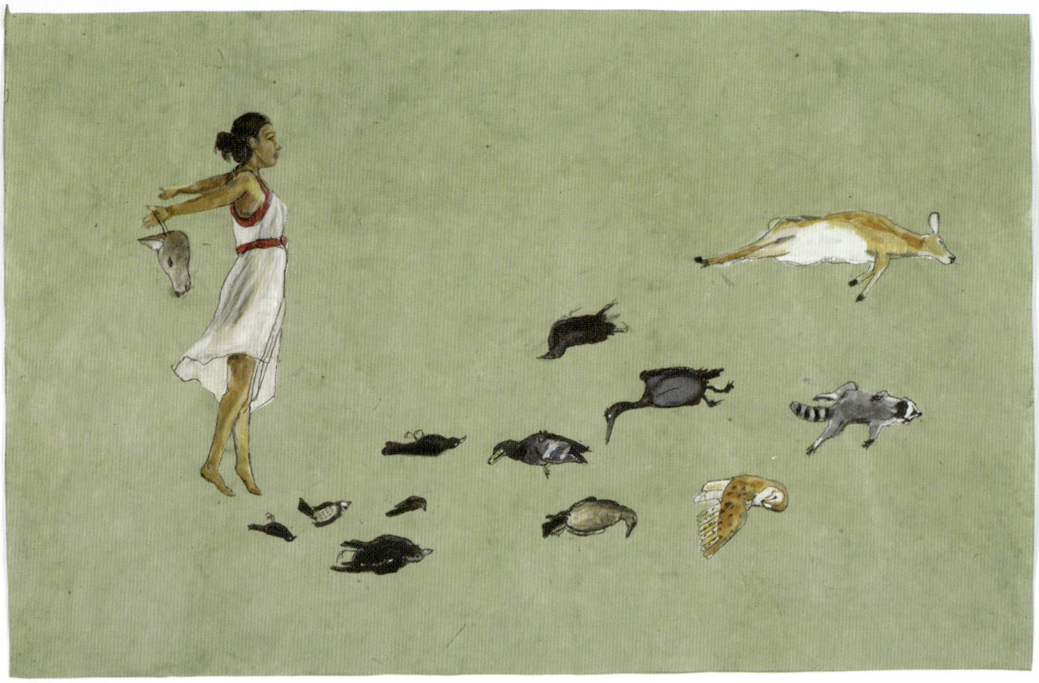

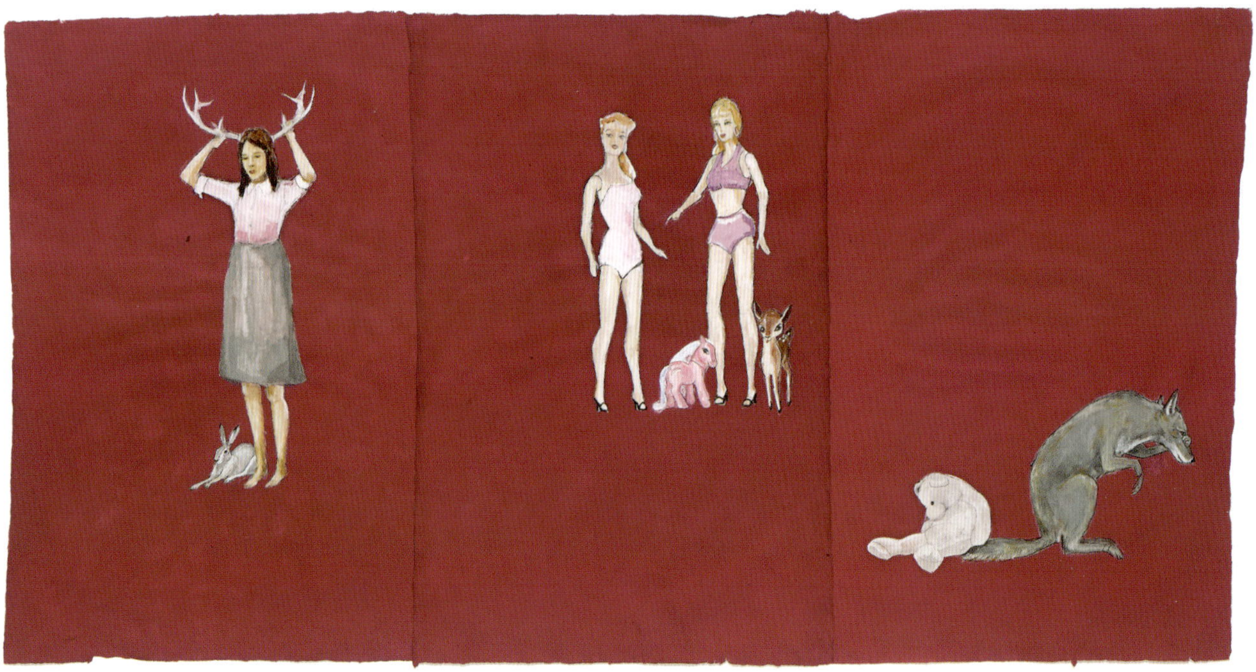

(Above) *The Medusa Syndrome*, 2010. Mixed media on paper. Image courtesy the Bockley Gallery. (Below) *My Life as Performed by Coyote, Rabbit, and Various Toys*, 2012. Mixed media on paper.

I think the matte surface allows for emphasis on the stories—and this sort of horizonless spatial treatment changes the pictorial context from my previous work—it becomes a mythic space, which has a feel that is different from the pictorial notions of perspective and foreshortening that Western European painting shows.[10]

Buffalohead's self-image is played out in *The Medusa Syndrome* and *My Life as Performed by Coyote, Rabbit and Various Toys*. In *The Medusa Syndrome*, the mask serves as a shield. It is a barrier that allows us to believe we are free from the confines of our own beliefs, whether imposed by society or our own insecurities: We are hidden, we are free. Alas, once the mask is lifted, the fear remains and the mundane dulling pain endures. "The woman removes her mask, revealing the true self, but everyone has turned to stone at the sight of her."[11]

In *My Life as Performed by Coyote, Rabbit and Various Toys*, Buffalohead again presents the myth of the idyllic childhood. It recalls the weight she bore as a child and must bear again as a mother knowing her daughter is susceptible to the same cruelties of the playground that she endured and that are a microcosm of our society.

This is an autobiographical piece about being ostracized with animals as my only friends. I was trying [to] illustrate young girls and their obsession with body image by taking Barbie dolls, blowing the toys up life-sized. The dolls are the instigators; they are more menacing than an innocent toy. They are destructive, toting their unrealistic expectations of body image. A coyote tears up from pain. It represents my being bullied as a child and the harm it has caused me.[12]

The antithesis of Buffalohead's painful experiences in childhood, as she reveals them through the metaphors of her paintings, is the courage she displays by her admission. She becomes a heroine of the front yard, the bathroom, and the wading pool she sets as her stage. Her pain is real, but her fortitude and perseverance are real as well. Through them, she becomes our champion, our triumph, in the agreement that "they" were wrong. Buffalohead's message is a private victory for all who share her pain.

The idea of Pocahontas, the exotic and stoic Indian, still persists. To demonstrate these persistent and inaccurate images of Native people, Buffalohead renders *Seems You Have to Play Indian to Be Indian*.

In this piece, I had a group of children playing cowboys and Indians with their tipis and tents. On the surface, it has a broader political significance, but underneath, it relates to my read on others' perceived ambivalence toward my own Indian identity—a frustration with society determining what native identity is, as is evident through one's appearance. For example, that Indians ought to have long braids, dark skin, and feathers. These stereotypes still persist.[13]

Buffalohead's desire to find the place where she "fits" takes her work through examinations of motherhood, beauty, love, and society's expectations in these areas as well as her connection to her Ponca culture. These issues have a culmination or accumulation in work like *The Love Object* and *If You Can't Love the One You're With*, which deal with the challenges and comfort realized in being biracial and in relationships with marked and defining differences.

[In The Love Object] there is a real rabbit holding a stuffed rabbit that is holding a traditional Native doll. This piece reminds me of being biracial and longing to be accepted. The real rabbit derives comfort from the stuffed one and the stuffed rabbit finds comfort from the doll.

Intimate, deeply felt, and usually secret feelings of longing are the subject of *If You Can't Love the One You're With*. It is "a story of unrequited love where rabbits each love a deer but the deer love each other."[14] Here

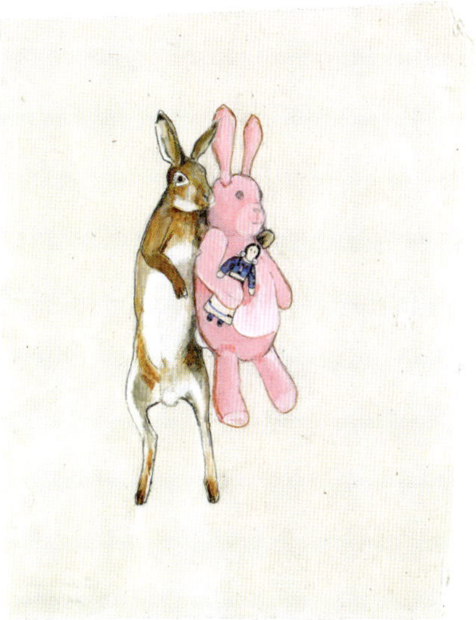

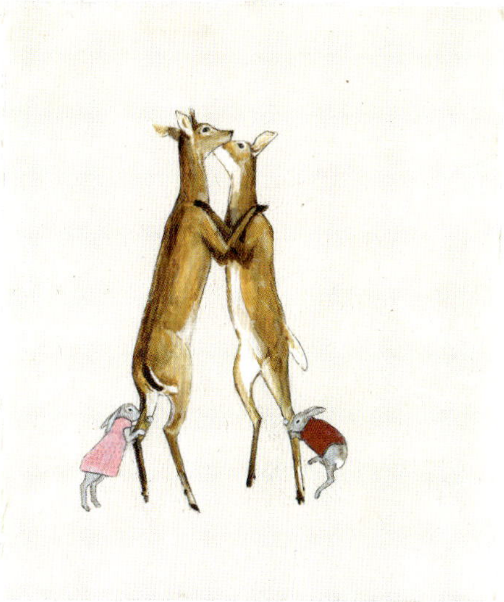

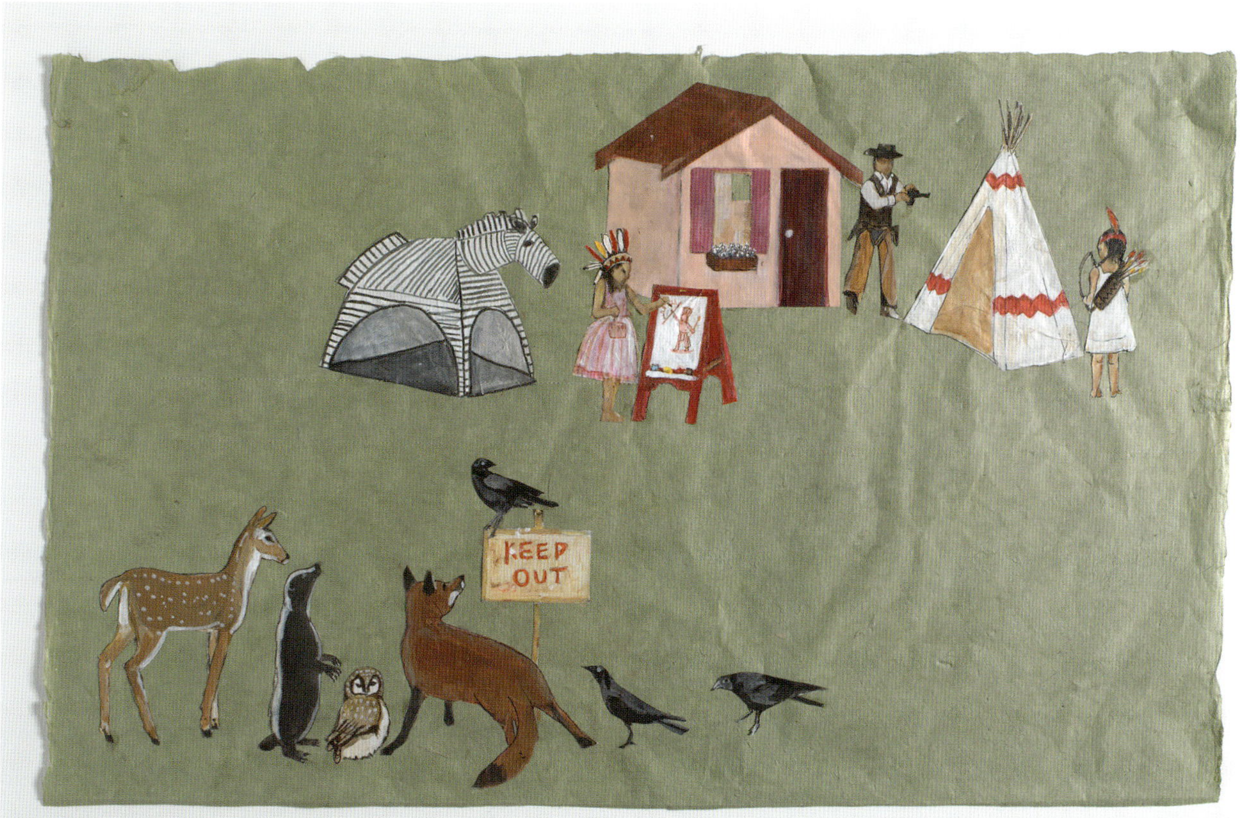

(Above left) *The Love Object*, 2012. Mixed media on paper. Image courtesy the Bockley Gallery. (Above right) *If You Can't Love the One You're With*. (Below) *Seems You Have to Play Indian to Be Indian*, 2010. Mixed media on paper. Image courtesy National Museum of the American Indian, Smithsonian Institution (268625.000). Photo by NMAI Photo Services.

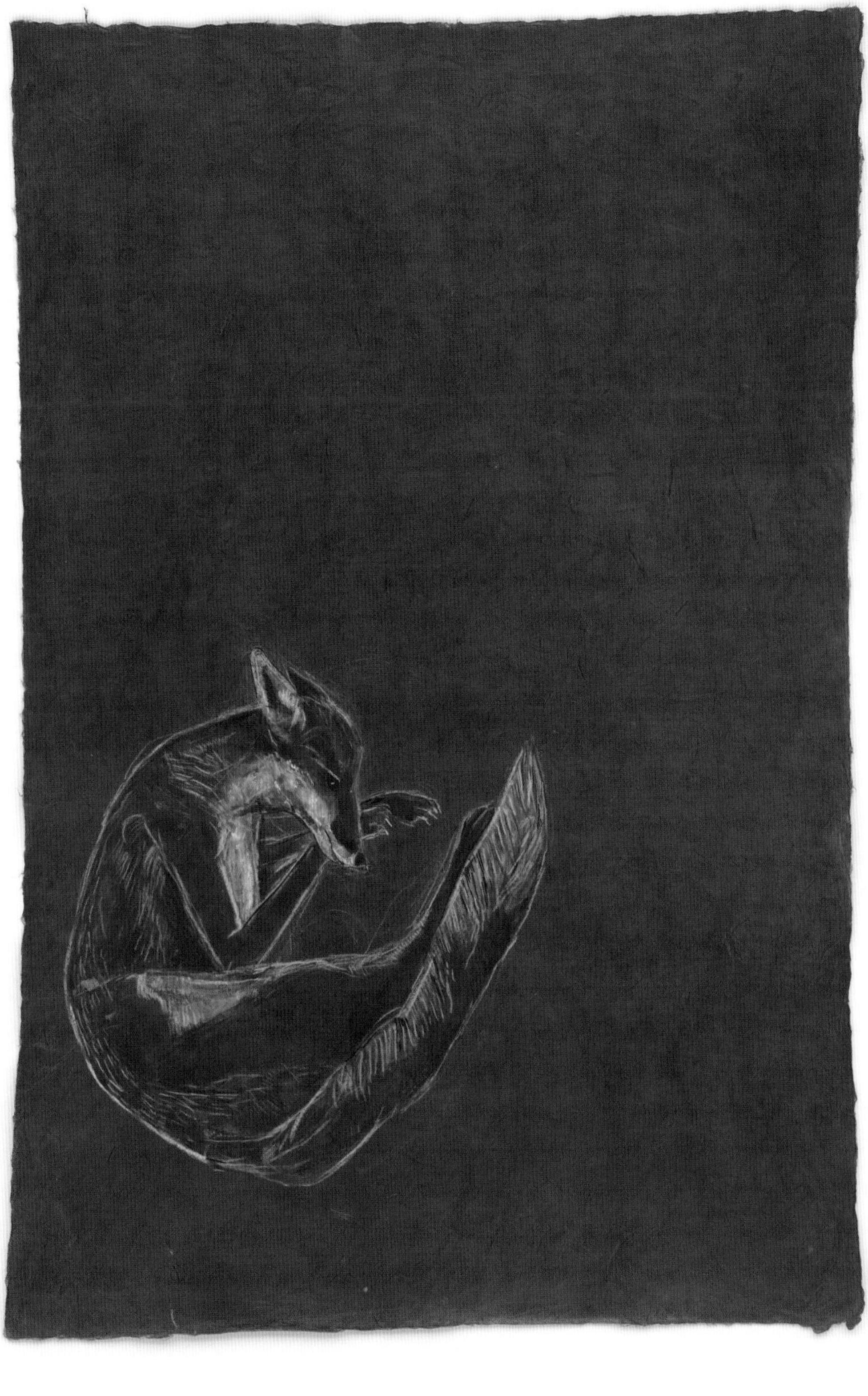

Heart Sick, 2012. Mixed media on paper. Image courtesy the Bockley Gallery.

Buffalohead may be examining issues of a biracial person or biracial relationships and the challenges and rewards they allow. The rabbits are unable to fulfill their desire for the deer, a species that bears little resemblance to them. Although their feeding habits are similar and they make their homes in similar settings, the rabbits look as though they fit together and the deer fit together. A deer/rabbit partnership creates logistical, as well as emotional, challenges. They speak different languages. The deer must bend into an awkward and uncomfortable position to look the rabbit in the eyes, to say nothing of the challenges their offspring would have in this world of stereotypes and preconceived conventions. However, the logic and social taboos of the situation are unlikely to be realized where the heart is concerned.

Beyond the unique and personal way Buffalohead approaches formal issues of painting and drawing is her emotional openness. A hallmark of her work is her willingness to examine with her stories the deep and private feelings that many of us share with only the closest of our friends or family. In *Heartsick*, an intimacy is revealed through the care of mark-making in the transparent drawing of the coyote that is disappearing into the paper and his unique and deliberate compositional positioning.

This bird's-eye view of a resting coyote fades into the background as he begins his transition into being invisible, a desirable state when one's heart is broken and the desire to fight dissipates. However, considering he is positioned facing upward on the vertical plane of paper, the pressure of his own weight will eventually force him to recover physically, if not emotionally, to a standing position, even if, uncharacteristically for Buffalohead's work , this coyote stands on all fours instead of in an upright biped position.

Buffalohead pulls no punches with her little-girl settings of a world made up of animals and reenacted events. Emotional and intimate, she is without pride in her pursuit of righting the wrongs that imposed impossible expectations on her as a child, grown woman, artist, and Native. She is formidable in her determination to overcome these wrongs by exposing them for what they are: unachievable, undesirable ways of making a dominant culture imposing and impenetrable. What a blow when it is revealed no one is coming to that playground any longer.

To persevere and overcome the oppressive pressure, one has to come to some resolution or acceptance. We find some of that refuge in *Reconcile*. In one way or another, we all must reconcile ourselves to even the most unpleasant, heartbreaking, and infuriating of experiences to move forward and keep the story alive and evolving and to triumph. Finding that reconciliation, that triumph, may be understanding, victory, laughter, tears, or, as Buffalohead states, "forgiveness," the most humbling and powerful emotion of all.

Kay WalkingStick wrestles with the emotional psychology, mystery, and importance of indigenous memory in Buffalohead's work.[15]

There was a profundity in the earliest paintings that I saw: a woman with a wolf's or coyote's head which was a frightening but very convincing image of what seemed to me one's (her?) inner self. Here was an image of a woman/wolf looking at the world with wild, wary animal eyes. We women can be strong, fearless & fearsome sometimes and fragile, too. Is that what the meaning of those paintings was?

The notion of man/animal beings is often seen in Native American imagery—think masks, pottery, & dance regalia. And it is also part of the mythic history of people around the world like the Etruscans, Greeks, Egyptians, and tribal people everywhere. Usually people take on the animal personae to imbue themselves with the strength, wisdom, and cunning of the beastie. Her early paintings certainly did take on a mythic power—the power of the animal in us to understand the great unknown, unanswerable questions of life on earth.

And for its mystery, my favorite painting is one called The Stand-off. It depicts a wolf/coyote holding a chicken above other chickens who are dressed as Plains Indians. (They are in Plains regalia.)

For me, this one is the most intriguing & frightening work although I cannot pretend to understand it, and in a way, I don't want to do so. These works are definitely not kid stuff in spite of the Bambi figures and stuffed toys.[16]

The meek creatures and seemingly harmless settings Buffalohead chooses to illuminate critical social issues with monumental consequences to society and her personally are truly not for the faint of heart. And it is that heart that invigorates her meek creatures and mighty trickster with the fortitude to slay the beast, to be the victor if only for a moment and then again with her lasting legacy of characters on location.

---

[1]Julie Buffalohead, interview with author, July 22, 2013.
[2]Ibid.
[3]Buffalohead, interview with author, July 4, 2013.
[4]Ibid.
[5]Ibid.
[6]Ibid.
[7]Buffalohead, interview with author, July 22, 2013.
[8]Buffalohead, interview with author, July 4, 2013.
[9] Buffalohead, interview with author, July 22, 2013.
[10]Ibid.
[11]Ibid.
[12]Ibid.
[13]Ibid.
[14]Ibid.
[15]Kay WalkingStick (Cherokee) is a retired professor of art who taught at Cornell University for nearly twenty years. Her work is widely collected by museums and individuals. WalkingStick was one of the inaugural selectors for the Eiteljorg Contemporary Art Fellowship and the 2003 recipient of the Eiteljorg Contemporary Fellowship Distinguished artist award. For a full biography, go to www.kaywalkingstick.com.
[16]Kay WalkingStick, interview with author, July 15, 2013.

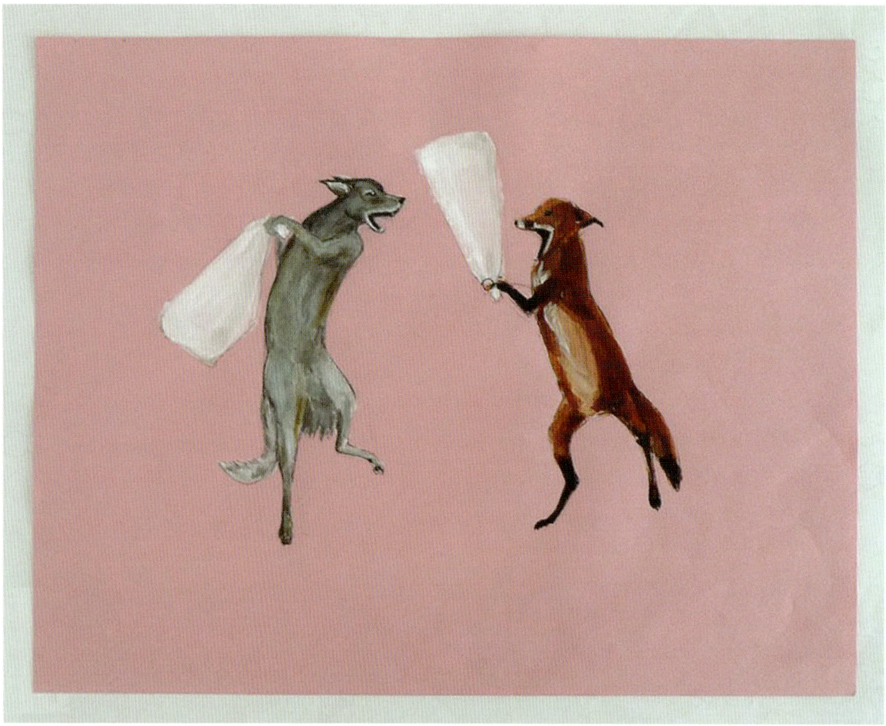

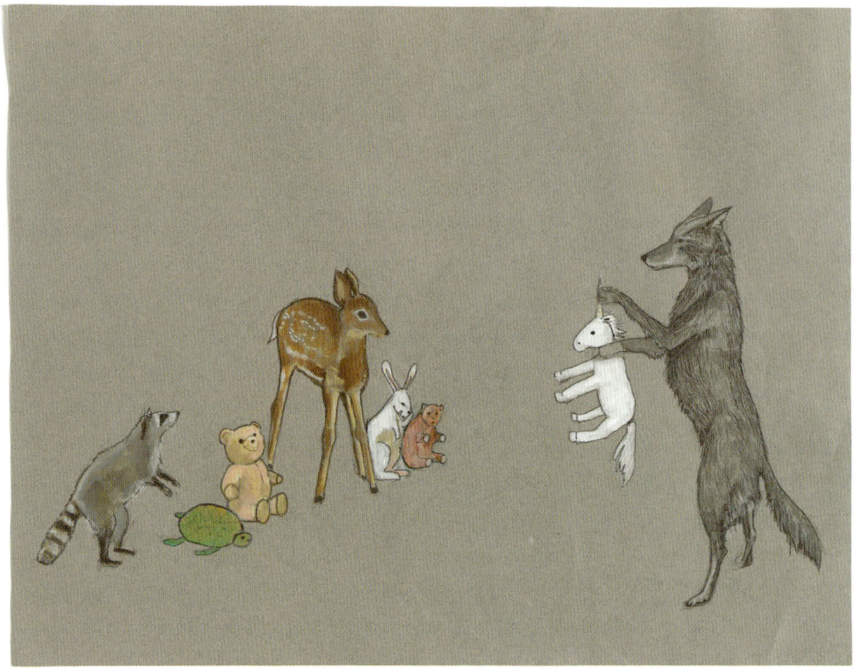

(Above) *Pillow Fight*, 2012. Mixed media on paper. Image courtesy the Bockley Gallery. (Below) *Hostage*, 2008. Mixed media on paper. Image courtesy National Museum of the American Indian, Smithsonian Institution (268626.000). Photo by NMAI Photo Services.

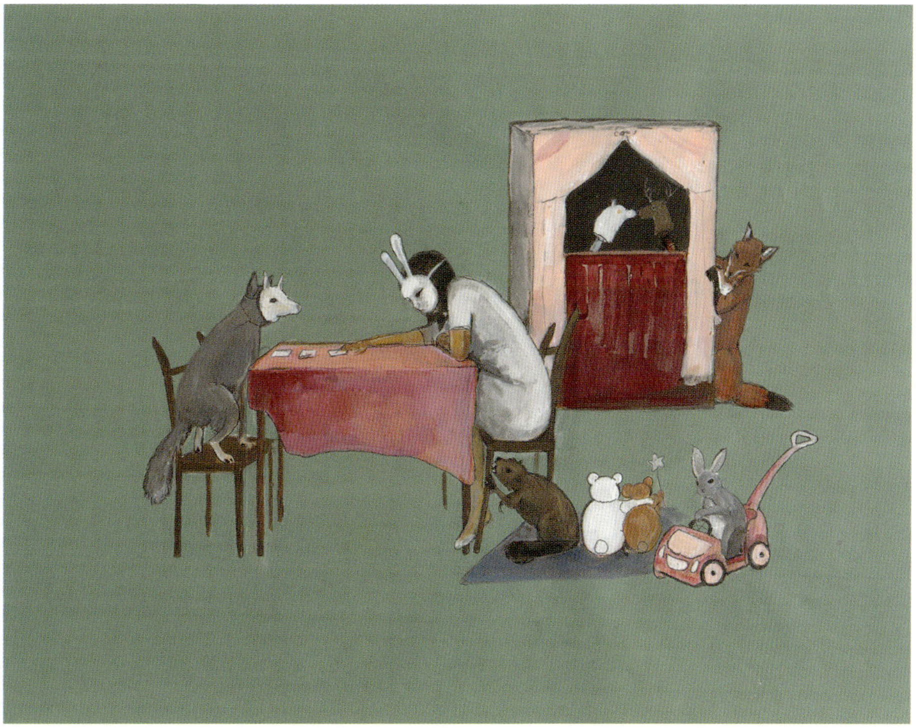

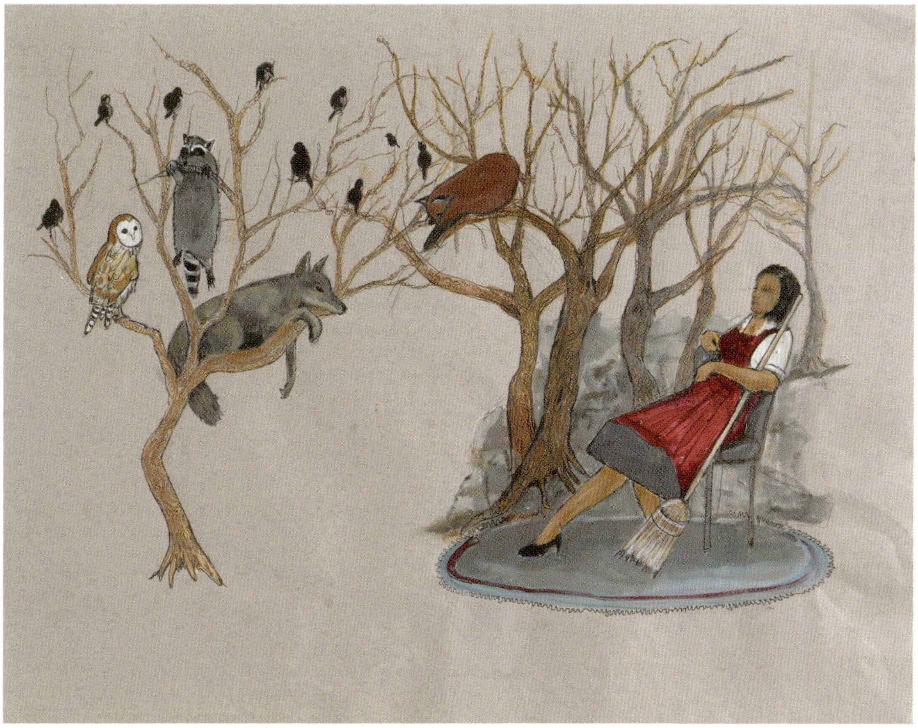

(Above) *Let the Show Begin*, 2010. Mixed media on paper. Image courtesy National Museum of the American Indian, Smithsonian Institution (268624.000). Photo by NMAI Photo Services. (Below) *The Spirit Trees*, 2010. Mixed media on paper. Image courtesy National Museum of the American Indian, Smithsonian Institution (268623.000). Photo by NMAI Photo Services.

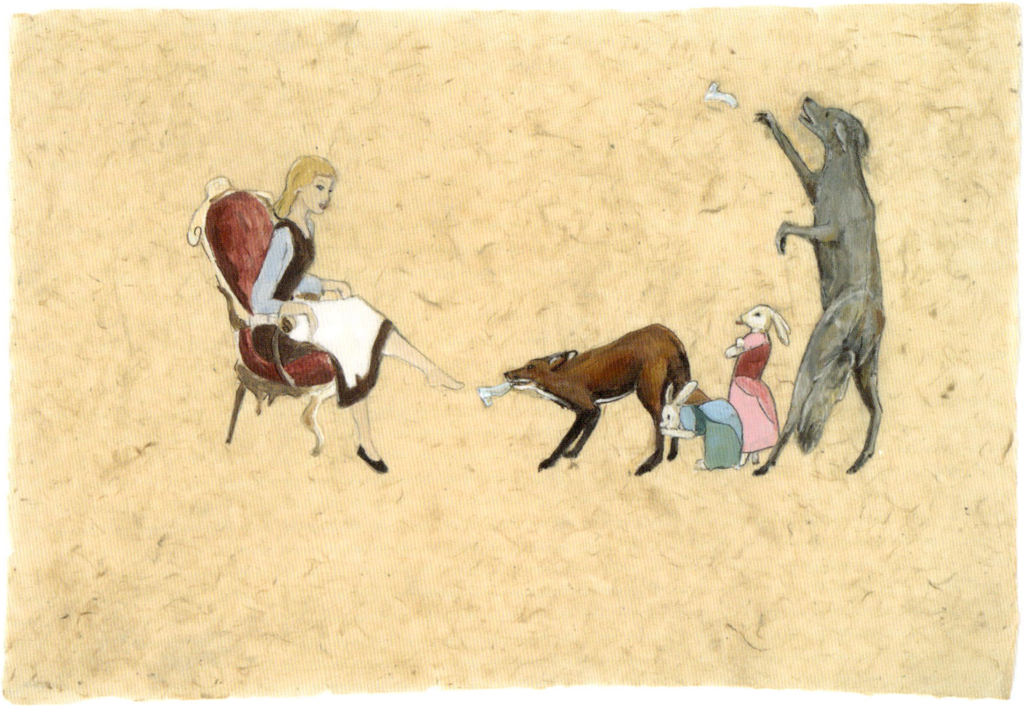

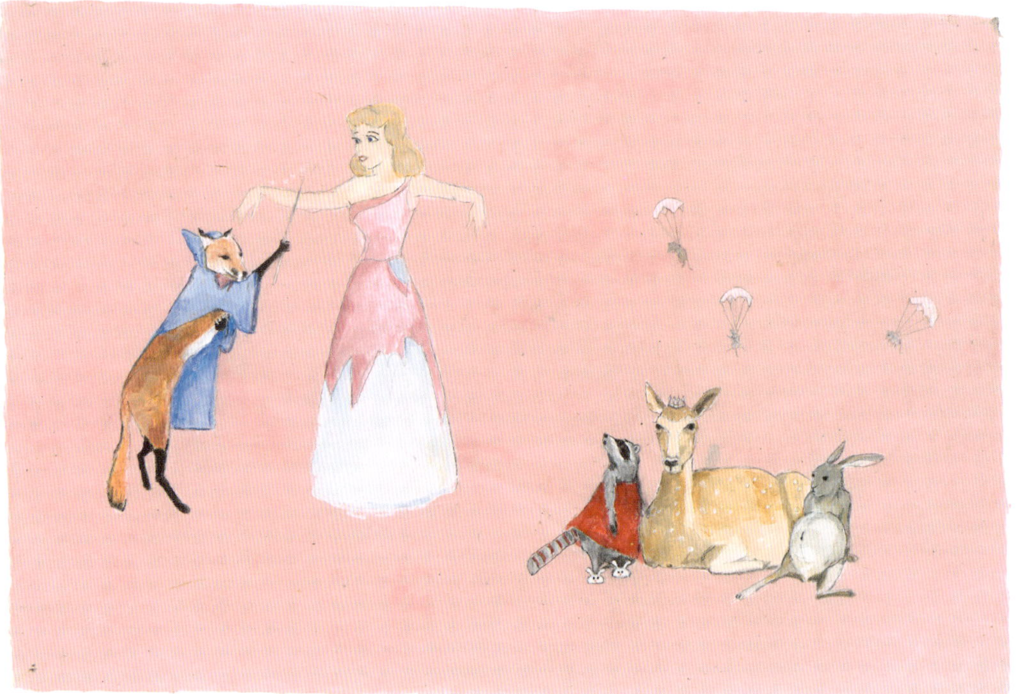

(Above) *The Little Glass Slipper,* 2012. Mixed media on paper. Image courtesy the Bockley Gallery. (Below) *Sometimes the Magic Works, Sometimes It Doesn't,* 2012. Mixed media on paper.

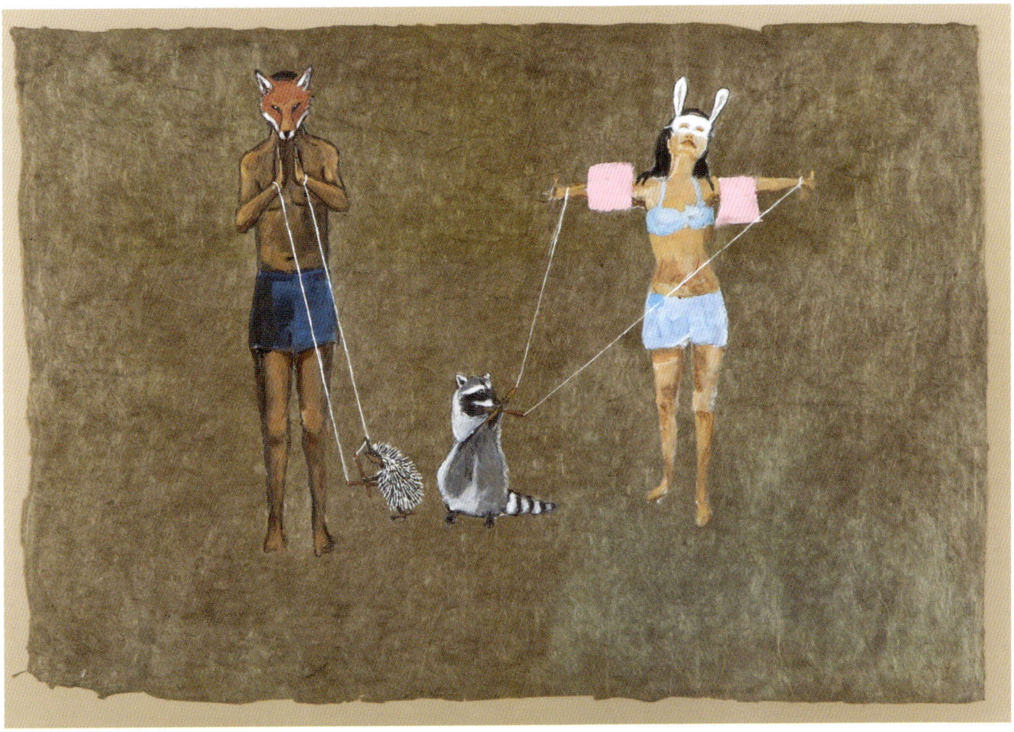

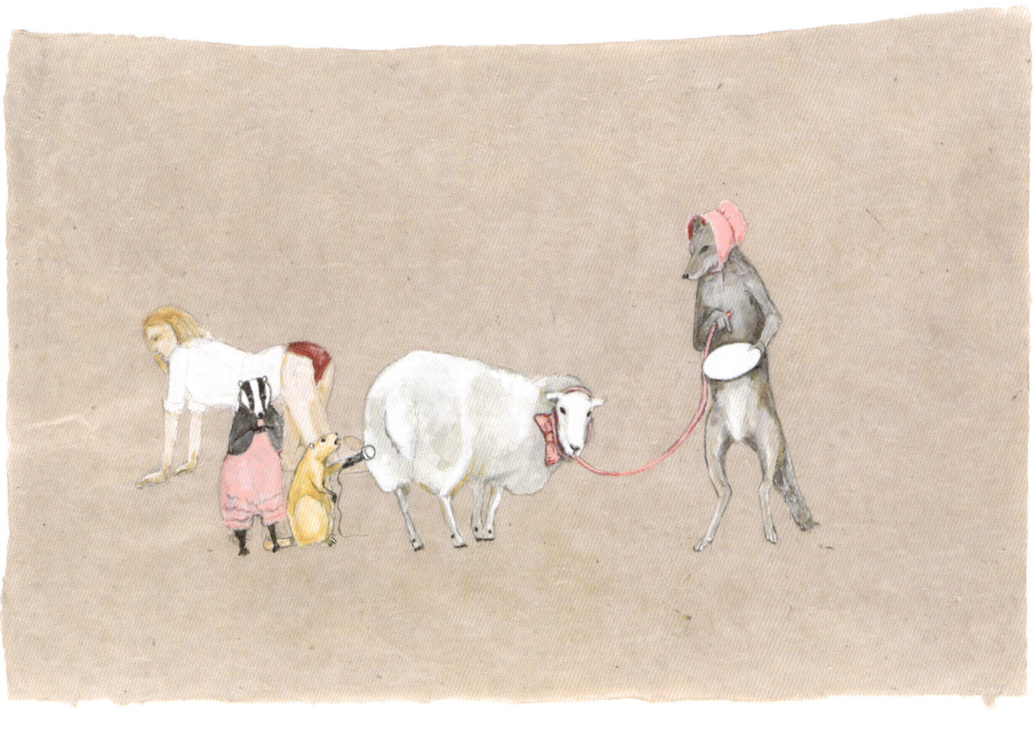

(Above) *I Feel This Much*, 2009. Mixed media on paper. (Below) *Little Boo Peep Forgot about her Sheep*, 2012. Mixed media on paper. Image courtesy the Bockley Gallery.

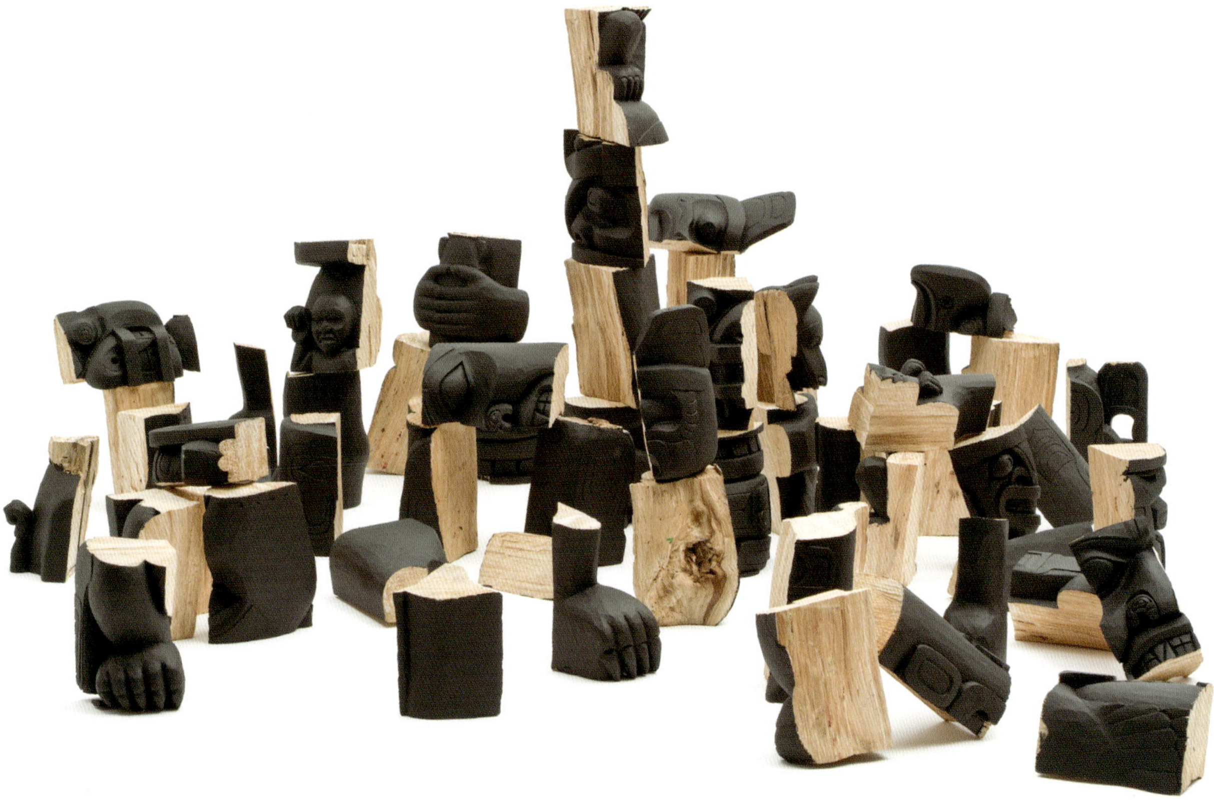

Nicholas Galanin, *I Think It Goes Like This?*, 2012. Wood, paint.

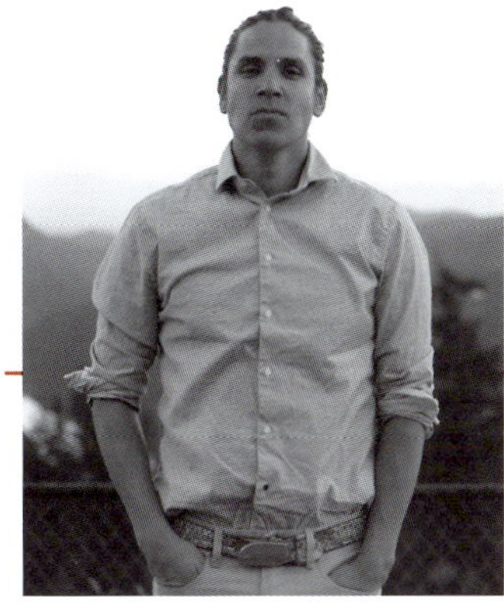

Nicholas Galanin

(Tlingit/Aleut)

Translate Transpose Transmit. Shifting Indigenous Aesthetics

Tania Willard (Secwepemc Nation)

Culture cannot be contained as it unfolds. My art enters this stream at many different points, looking backwards, looking forwards, generating its own sound and motion.

k̲aa ji.eetí: handiwork, artifact (n). **yakwteiyí:** tricks, sleight of hand (n)

These words are Tlingit nouns that were identified simply by typing *trick* and *art* into an online Tlingit dictionary.[1] The role of new media in preserving and storing indigenous languages online is a current and complicated phenomenon. The translations may or may not be accurate, and if the source does not include audio files, then pronunciation is a mystery. Digitized methods and efforts to archive and renew indigenous languages and cultural knowledge remind us that indigenous arts and cultures are always shifting and that within that shift, we may experience loss. We might learn words in indigenous languages from an online source as opposed to hearing our grandmothers speak them, but we also may gain new insights, possibilities, and opportunities to regain culture through non-traditional methods. The spaces between Internet data and grandmothers' voices seem vast, but indigenous artists like Nicholas Galanin frame this shifting terrain of indigeneity in ways that posit new narratives, cultural shift, and digital methods while maintaining strong roots.

Alaskan-based Tlingit artist Nicholas Galanin's work is a poignant example of straddling the remarkable interstice between traditional and contemporary art. The aesthetic classifications of "craft," "contemporary," and "traditional" and/or "Native art" all conjure particular sets of expectations. Galanin's work plays with these expectations. His work travels two parallel paths. One path follows an expected trajectory in traditional carving and jewelry that his great-grandfather passed to his father. The second path veers off dramatically with inquiry into satire and iconoclasm, and encompasses more of the artist's "contemporary" art practice seen in museums and galleries. However, the expected signifiers of cultural object or ethnographic art are undermined in his practice by the conceptual nature of his process. By outsourcing the production of some of his work, Galanin subverts the idea of the folkloric Indian artist and replaces that narrative with a sense of globalized craft that carries into Indian art and wider culture. Referencing and exploiting the interplay of art, culture, and commerce, Galanin's work examines shifting cultures as if they were tectonic plates, the monumental movement within them creating faults, mountains, and earthquakes as cultures assimilate, adapt, and expropriate.

When I first curated Galanin's work at an exhibition during an Aboriginal Curatorial Collective conference in Vancouver, BC (2008), I was struck by the way in which the artist navigated prescriptive ideas about Native art and explored further possibilities of indigenous art, inquiry, and aesthetic. A year or so after this exhibition, I attended a curatorial excursion to the 2010 Sydney Biennale and spent some time in Aotearoa (New Zealand), where I met with indigenous artists and curators. It was on this trip that I met Maori artists and curators who told me about their work and associations with Nicholas and the time he had spent at Massey University, where he earned his master's degree in indigenous visual arts. His work in Aotearoa was memorable. For his graduating exhibition, he brought in a sign that read, "No Indians or Dogs Allowed." The piece was an investigation of historical and current prejudice and policies of persistent racism against indigenous people in the artist's home of Alaska and globally. This work also included a neon sign that was placed in storefronts, an assertion of current political climates and a foray into new materials and media that was suggestive of the development of the artist's later work. Nicholas' studies at Massey University perhaps equipped him with an understanding of similarities and differences in global indigenous arts culture. He is particularly familiar with Maori contemporary practice. Maori artists incorporate Maori

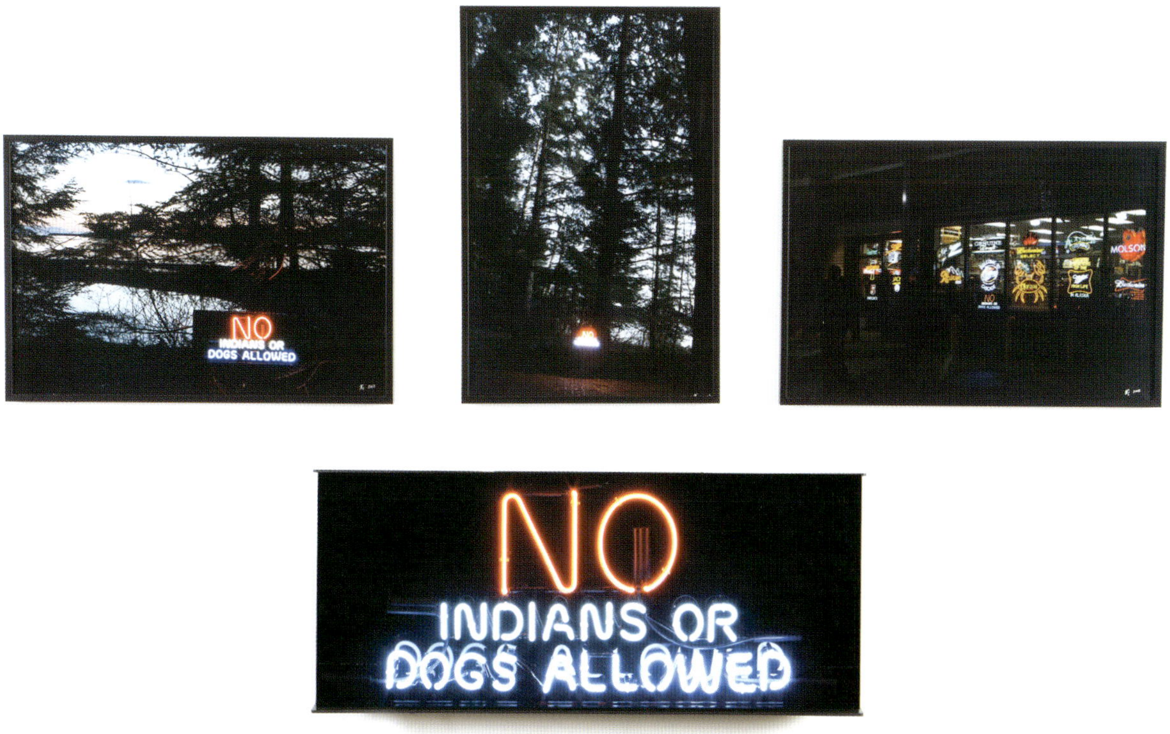

No Indians or Dogs Allowed, 2008. Neon, photography.

cosmology into works that maintain a connection to cultural practice but also comment on and engage with current politics, technologies, and popular culture. Galanin's work is informed by globalized cultures, freedom of cultural expression, and the manifestations of change in a world of shifting cultures and ancestral echoes.

"Traditional" is a term often misused in most indigenous scenes. While in New Zealand, I noticed the Maori people's eloquence with cultural representation through their second language, English. The preferred term was "customary." To me, this term allows for more than one way of being. To preserve a culture's customs, whether it be language, politics, or the arts, is very rewarding and necessary, just as crucial as growth and progress are.[2]

His earlier body of work *What Have We Become?* and the video works *Tsu Heidei Shugaxtutaan (We will again open up this container of wisdom that has been left in our care) I* and *II* are iconic visualizations of the push and pull between seemingly paradoxical viewpoints and practices of customary art, cultural preservation, and contemporary practice. The two-part video contrasts a Tlingit raven mask-dance with a digitized electronic music soundtrack and Tlingit drum song with a contemporary dancer. Representing in some ways a younger generation of indigenous artists, Galanin is conscious of cultural protocols. While he recognizes the importance of custom on a cultural level, he is also a risk taker. In past artist's statements, Galanin has talked about the impact of his work on members of his community and an older generation of artists. In some instances, this work does not translate, but he says it is still a part of him as a complete person with varied cultural expressions and influences. Previous generations of indigenous artists had to fight to keep their arts, traditions, cultures, and languages alive. While that fight continues in many ways, a younger generation of artists has emerged. These individuals are more informed about their cultural heritage, but they have many other influences, and denying these influences denies the existence of contemporary indigenous people as whole, diverse and self-defining. What Galanin does in *Tsu Heidei*

Shugaxtutaan I and *II* is position indigenous culture as a continuum as opposed to two fixed points, traditional and contemporary. I only recently learned that in the second part of the video, the beautifully carved Northwest coast background was carved in part by Galanin with other more senior carvers and family members. This tidbit adds even more dimension to the artist's conflating and juxtaposing these ideas.In doing so, he asserts a continuum of culture and ideas, of a living, dynamic group of culture(s). His own Tlingit culture is part of that. Importantly, this continuum is cyclical, not an evolution or progress toward modern or post-modern contemporary art. What Galanin's work suggests is that culture is shifting. We are translating and adapting, the same as our ancestors did and as our grandchildren will do, and that is what creates our cultures.

Being brought up both in and away from my indigenous culture, I have experienced a very different perspective on my heritage than my great-grandparents would have known. The generational spread that our cultural community encompasses moves far beyond a romantic ideal commonly associated with the term "Indian Art." We are being culturally dishonest if we reject all that passes through our culture.[3]

Raven and the First Immigrant, a chainsaw-carved piece in the collection of the University of British Columbia's Museum of Anthropology, is also an important work within Galanin's oeuvre. Drawing on his mentorship in Northwest Coast carving, this work is a crude interpretation of Bill Reid's masterwork. Protocol and restrictions in Northwest Coast art can be very defined. Other important artists have commented on the balance between individual freedom of expression and artistic tradition or customary practice. Lawrence Paul Yuxweluptun's *Haida Hot Dog* approaches this debate with the same irreverent attitude as Galanin's, but both artists are also still very much grounded in the knowledge of more customary practices. The old adage to know the rules before breaking them seems to be central. Importantly, in *Raven and the First Immigrant*, Galanin did not carve the

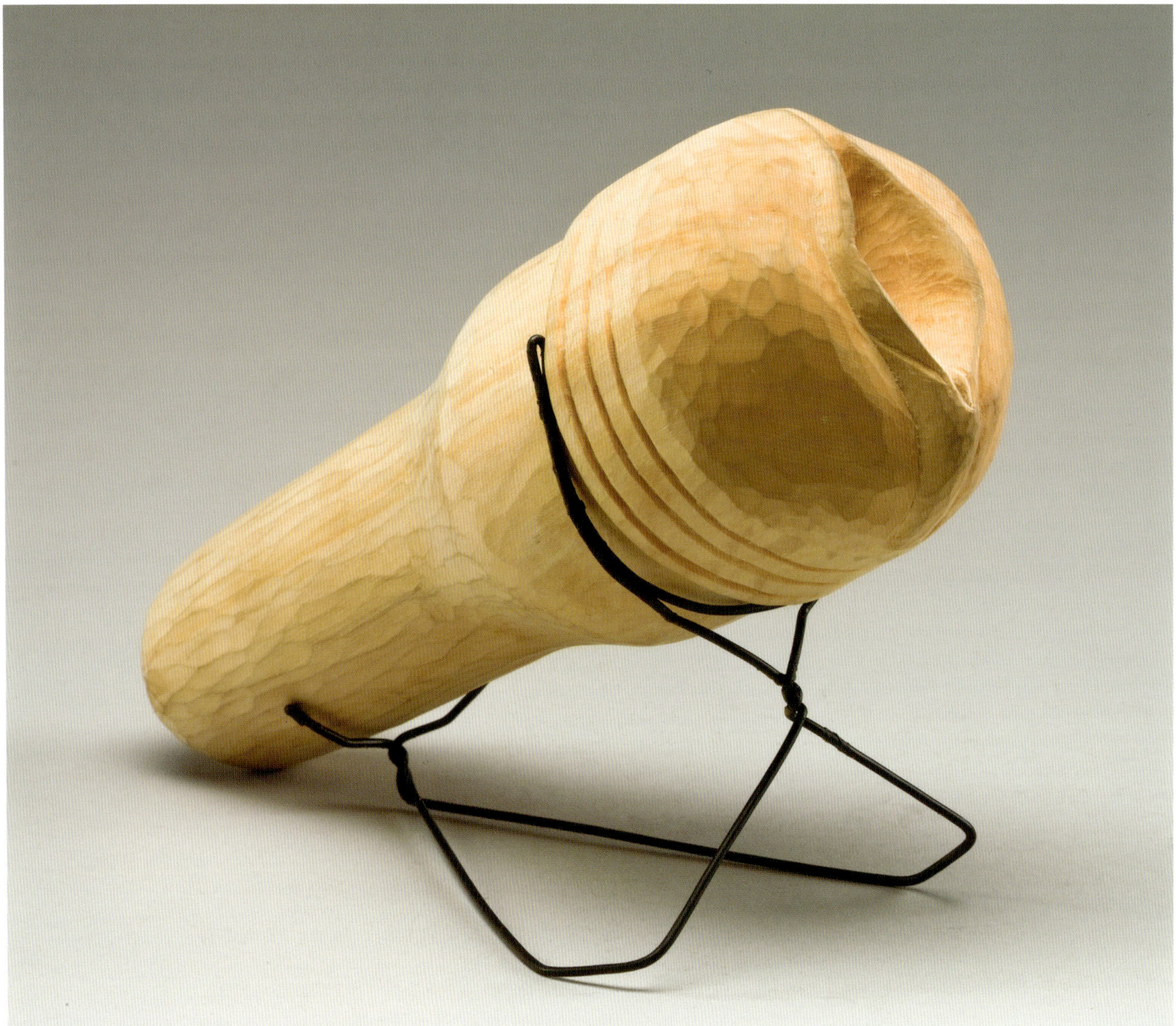

I Looooove Your Culture! Fine Wood Working, 2012. Yellow cedar.

work—he had a non-Native Seattle-based chainsaw carver create it. In this case, the process of the work is very much a part of the piece. In Alaska, the number of tourist items represented as being made by Native artists, but that are actually made by non-Natives, is great. Many of Galanin's works comment on the commodity nature of Native art, and in *Raven and the First Immigrant*, this is certainly the case. In a solo exhibition, *I Looooove Your Culture*, at Trench Gallery (2012), Galanin went even further and had a non-Native carver working in the corner of the gallery. This installation, *White Carver,* directly confronts the globalized production (Northwest Coast masks carved in Indonesia, for example) and mythic nature of the Native carver. This mimesis of the inauthentic in turn is a warning. Commodity-based cultural representation is confronted by the artist and the viewer. The non-Native carver hired by Galanin to be a part of this exhibition is claimed by the artist and becomes authentically inauthentic. Some of Galanin's pieces are in fact carved by the non-Native carver, but this information is not always explicitly outlined in the work. The debate about the authenticity of Native art is delicate. Native artists in Alaska are protected by the Silver Hand Program™, which measures the level of an authentically made Alaskan Native art product. While one can view these types of programs as helpful, ensuring that Native artists are compensated for their work and that global production of Indian icons in China, Taiwan, and Indonesia is kept at bay, Galanin instead embraces and appropriates these artifacts, complete with their tales of global cultural capital and the commodification of the sacred, and exposes them by using them as a medium, the global production of Indian kitsch.

Economics and cultural objects, curio and collector, Indians and museum, history and the present. I often like to unravel the things that irritate the Indian in me, putting them back on the shelf with new meaning, clarity or focus. As an artist that contributes to my culture, I feel immense gratitude knowing that I am able to give to something greater, this feeling of belonging is the Indian Art World.[4]

An earlier series of Galanin's work titled *The Imaginary Indian* sets about breaking all the rules of Northwest Coast art, juxtaposing Indonesian-manufactured Northwest Coast-style masks and French toile wallpaper. Galanin explores the authentic and inauthentic and how interpretation, appropriation, and cultural drift inform Northwest Coast art. In his series of slipcast ceramic masks, *s'igeikáawu: ghost*, Galanin appropriates an Indonesian mask that has been carved in Northwest Coast style and reconfigures it in ceramic with delftware patterning. The ceramic masks resonate with colonial ceramic traditions, but in Galanin's exploration, the decorative and pastoral elements in the delftware patterning and French toile wallpaper become a pox on the faces of the masks. They become afflicted, not decorated. The carved mask resonates with symbology, ceremony, and tradition in many cultures, certainly in Tlingit culture, and in Northwest Coast artistic practice, the mask is a ubiquitous art object. Galanin's exploration of masks can be seen in a number of his works. They form the foundation of Galanin's solo exhibition, *Oblique Drift* (grunt gallery, 2010, Vancouver, BC and MOCNA, 2010, Santa Fe, NM). The series *What Have We Become?* also includes masks and portraits made from the pages of the Bible and/or sculpted out of bound volumes of text and pages. These three-dimensional works jut out from the pages of books, asserting presence and coming alive as if to confront a viewer. This sense of confrontation can also be seen in a later work, *Inert*, in which Nicholas displays a half-stuffed, half-rug taxidermy wolf. The wolf is positioned with the front torso and legs in an upright position and the back half flattened out like a bear skin rug. This position animates the wolf so that it appears to be coming alive, suggesting a revenge or resurrection. His work with animal skin and taxidermy can also be seen in recent works. *The American Dream is Alie and Well* is a sort of lodge-like, splayed-out animal skin rug, but instead of a skinned animal, Nicholas has skinned the nation-state. The American flag forms the entire skin of this bear, and its claws are made from .50 caliber bullets. *Polar Bear Welcome Mat* is another work in this vein, a satirical doormat. The glistening polar bear fur contrasts with the dark sea otter fur letters that spell out "Welcome" in a seemingly hand-stitched font. Ideas of authenticity, production, and craft are apparent in many of Nicolas Galanin's works: His work *The Imaginary Indian*, a series of Tlingit-styled masks carved

(Right) *The American Dream is Alie and Well* (detail), 2012. United States flag, felt, .50 caliber blank cartridges, foam, gold leaf, plastic.

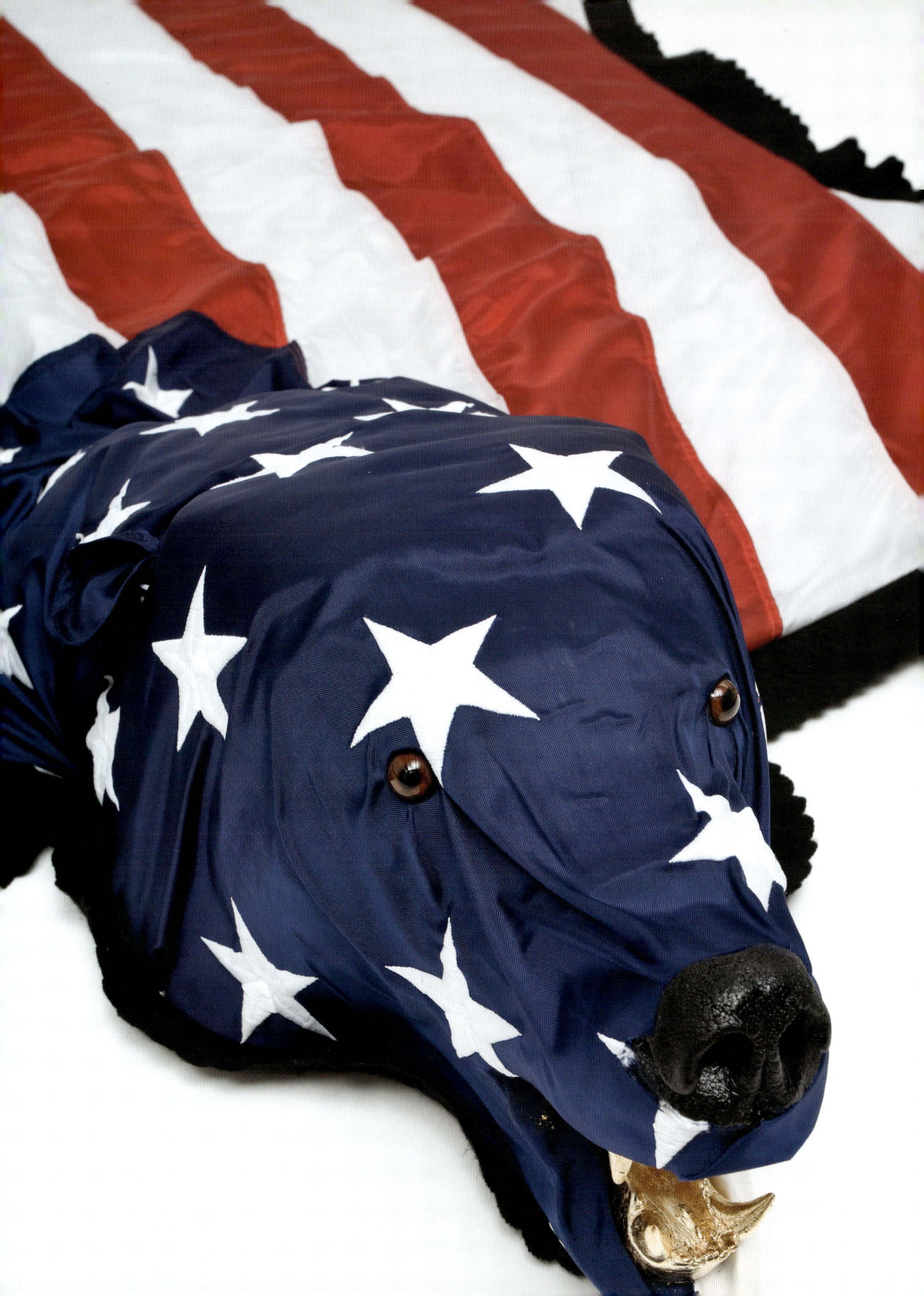

in Indonesia, comments on globalization and informs other works. In *Polar Bear Welcome Mat*, these ideas of craft, as well as the use of animal skins once customarily used as clothing and now as trophies, and the traditions behind hunting are suspended in irony as we envision wiping our feet on this precious, endangered polar bear fur. The discourse on climate change (for which the polar bear is now the poster child) and the perceived threat of extinction of these animals are called up as an imagined sacrilege implicating the viewer. As we imagine the mat's intended use, we are left with a raw belly laugh that might end in tears.

Nicholas' petroglyph series were included in the precedent-setting exhibition *Sakhán* at the National Gallery of Canada (2013). In discussion during an interview, the curators of this exhibition framed the problematic nature of contextualizing indigenous arts practices as "contemporary" or not.

If the past is always present in the works of indigenous art, how do we define contemporary? I think what it does is it shifts out the understanding of contemporary to not just mean "this moment," to have a very surface sense of living in the immediacy. Instead, it looks at how this moment can always be informed by our actions before it. It's not about an idea of historical progress, but an idea that is always a cycle.[5]

Nicholas Galanin's practice is situated within this sense of cycle and balance. Despite the distinct paths his work follows, these separate paths of customary and contemporary art collide, swerve, and meet each other throughout the body of his work. The petroglyph works, one of which sits outside the side entrance to the Vancouver Art Gallery, are about this sense of continuum. Change is not a purveyor of progress necessarily, but rather is a way of life: controversy as dialogue, confrontation as possibility. These works are like the Cleveland Indians' logo, etched in stone with the word "INDIANS." What does this say to us, that cultural stereotype and injustice will be remembered? Or that the artist has transformed it by claiming a sense of ownership of this word steeped in ignorance, this mascot and logo embroiled in racism? It is this sense of irony and reclamation that Galanin positions his work to exploit. The artist's work with cultural signifiers like wood carving, craft, and animal skins takes us to a place of expectations—the Native carver, hunter, artist—but the artist's clever use of these materials leads us to surprising interpretations. In some ways, the artist acts as a translator, digesting popular culture and influence and adapting cultural meaning and aesthetic out of this material. Galanin's work with popular culture can be seen across his work, especially in works like *Things Are Looking Native, Natives Are Looking Whiter*, in which he reworks modern advertising, movie production, and historical iconic image. Princess Leia from *Star Wars* is shown in contrast to an Edward Curtis photograph of a young Hopi woman, and their hair styles are remarkably similar. What becomes evident is that popular culture borrows or steals a great deal from indigenous cultures. We need only to look at Disney classics like *Pocahontas* or modern blockbusters like *Avatar* to see how indigenous story is expropriated without attribution to any particular author, nation, or tribe.

Galanin has worked with the legacy of Edward Curtis images in other works. *The Curtis Legacy,* a very provocative and controversial piece, positions a pornographic nude wearing Indonesia-carved Northwest Coast-style masks in a series of five pin-up and pornographic poses. Galanin has been criticized for his loaded use of the objectification of the female body in these works. The artist is using this association to compare the objectification of a culture, the objectification of Native people through the lens of Edward Curtis. Galanin's deft balance of these issues may not be as strong in these works because the use of the female form can evoke so many other loaded responses. Another work in this vein is *I Looooove Your Culture! Fine Wood Working*, which is a pocket pussy or sex toy carved from yellow cedar by Galanin's stand-in non-Native carver. Here Galanin has again used the extreme and pornographic objectification of the female body to indicate the commodification and exploitation of indigenous cultures. The artist references this work along with the *White Carver* installation wherein the carver is replicating a work carved by Galanin. The abuse and appropriation of cultural form are equated with the pornographic, wherein an image or a toy/body is used without any respect or attachment. While one can understand the artist's use of this theme and the comparison he

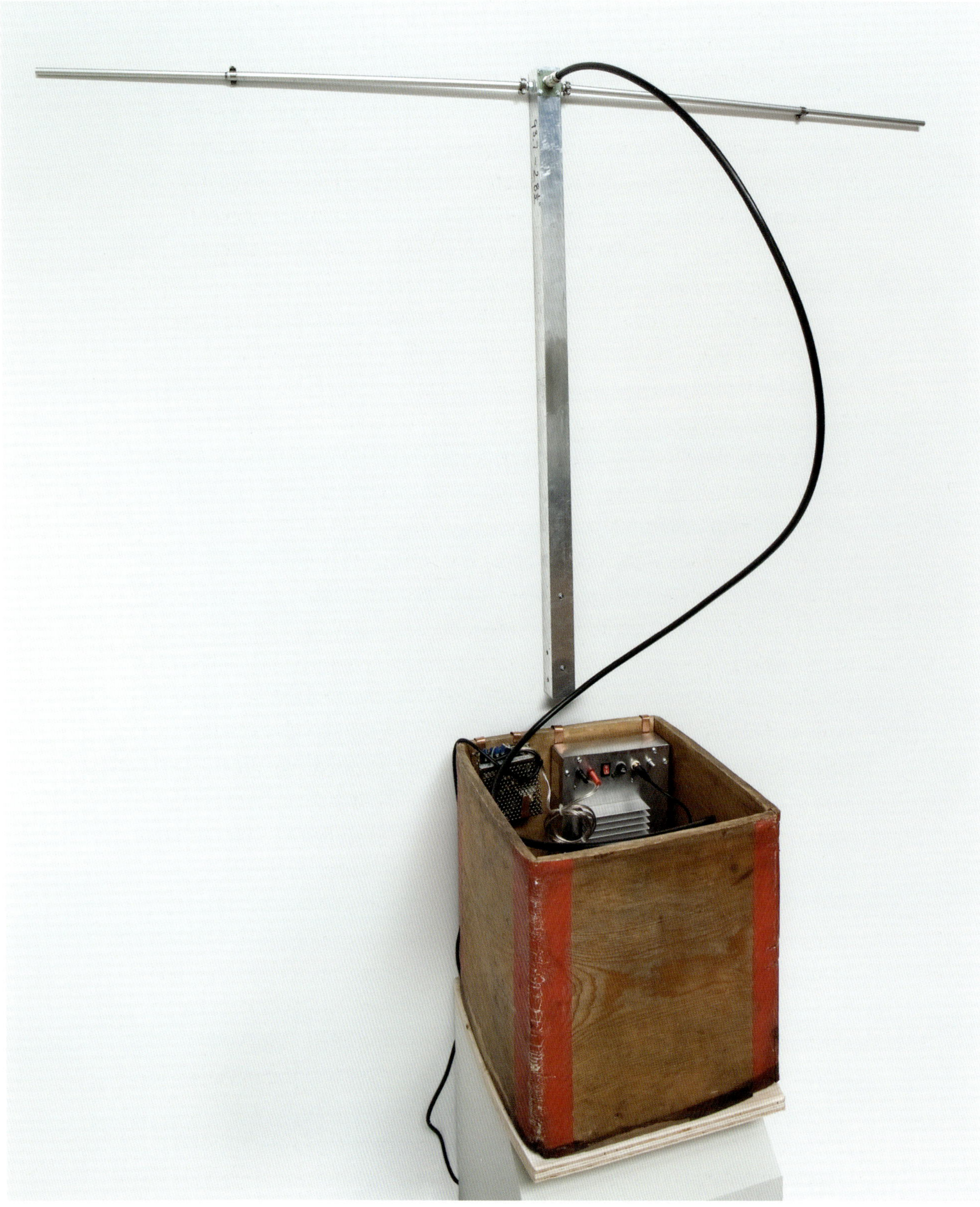

U'háan-We, 2012 [in collaboration with Jerrod Galanin as Leonard Getinthecar]. Radio Transmitter tuned to 93.7 broadcasting Tlingit language lessons, aluminum antenna, iPod shuffle, nineteenth-century Tlingit redcorner bentwood storage box.

is making, a feminist understanding of this work might further implicate the artist in the dialogue.

Galanin identifies a sense of romanticism in the exhibition and series of work *I Looooove Your Culture*, and transposes that romanticism into a critical and satirical look at the iconography of being Indian. An examination of the shifting nature of indigeneity can be seen in *I Think It Goes Like This*?, a seeming puzzle of dissected totem pole or sculptural elements, disassembled and installed as a pile of disparate but related elements. Painted matte black, the carving's protocol is all mixed up. Which clan animal goes where? The eagle is not on top. Is there even an eagle? Indians are all about eagles. The artist cuts up expectations and rule books in his push to question and innovate. As much as Galanin likes to mix up and target cultural stereotypes with satire, his work is also about having a big heart and a deep respect for his cultural heritage. It's hard to be an iconoclast in Indian Country. Tradition, ritual, and protocol are very real and diverse within different nations, but they are compounded by an internalized Disneyification or pan-Indian panacea: We take ourselves pretty seriously. Galanin's careful balance of satire and criticalness are measured with skill, heart, and humor—one of our strongest Indian medicines.

In the work *U'háan-We*, Galanin presents a radio transmitter tuned to 93.7 and broadcasting Tlingit language lessons from an iPod shuffle, inside a nineteenth-century Tlingit red-corner bentwood storage box. Galanin refers to the bentwood box as a collaboration with the ancestral, and states that this work in particular is also about reclamation, imagining a future embodied by ancestral knowledge and aesthetics and yet transformed by contemporary context. Indigenous artists are creating new contexts for considering the contemporary. Galanin is at the forefront of this wave, broadcasting Tlingit language and culture and translating that culture into forms that his ancestors might not recognize, but his grandchildren will remember. It is in that cultural memory full of innovation and adaptation, survival and struggle, humor and history that we locate colonialism and histories of injustice, but in which we can also locate the ways in which our ancestors continue to broadcast their teachings to us.

In the last few years, Galanin's work has garnered ever-increasing media attention and accolades. It is important to examine the ways in which mainstream or arts media are commenting on his body of work and on the artist himself. Largely reported or written about as someone who is transforming contemporary Native art or our expectations of Native art, these reports seem to also buy into ideas of some kind of evolution of Native art into contemporary art. This is expressly not the case in Galanin's work, in which what seems new is really a continuum. There is no post-modern or post-colonial in Indian country, but I recently read on my Facebook news feed that the original *Star Wars* was being translated into Navajo. This is the world now; it is important that we have artists who reflect our current realities back to us but do so without abandoning who we are within our diverse cultural identities. Native culture and Native art do not exist, but culture(s) and art(s) are thriving. Galanin mixes us up to set us right.

"The real strength in survival of indigenous knowledge and culture lies within the ability to freely and creatively represent ourselves."[6]

---

[1] "Alaska Native Language Interactive Dictionaries," accessed July 26, 2013, http://www.alaskool.org/language/dictionaries/akn/startdictionary.asp.

[2] Ronald Egger, "Nicolas Galain—Tlingit/Aleut," Contemporary North American Indigenous Artists, February 25, 2010, http://contemporarynativeartists.tumblr.com/post/479617639/nicholas-galanin-tlingit-aleut.

[3] Ibid.

[4] Ibid.

[5] Bryne McLaughlin, "Curator Q&A: How Indigenous Art Took Centre Stage in Sakahàn," http://www.canadianart.ca/features/2013/05/23/sakahan-national-gallery-of-canada/.

[6] Artist's statement for grunt gallery exhibition *Oblique Drift*, 2010.

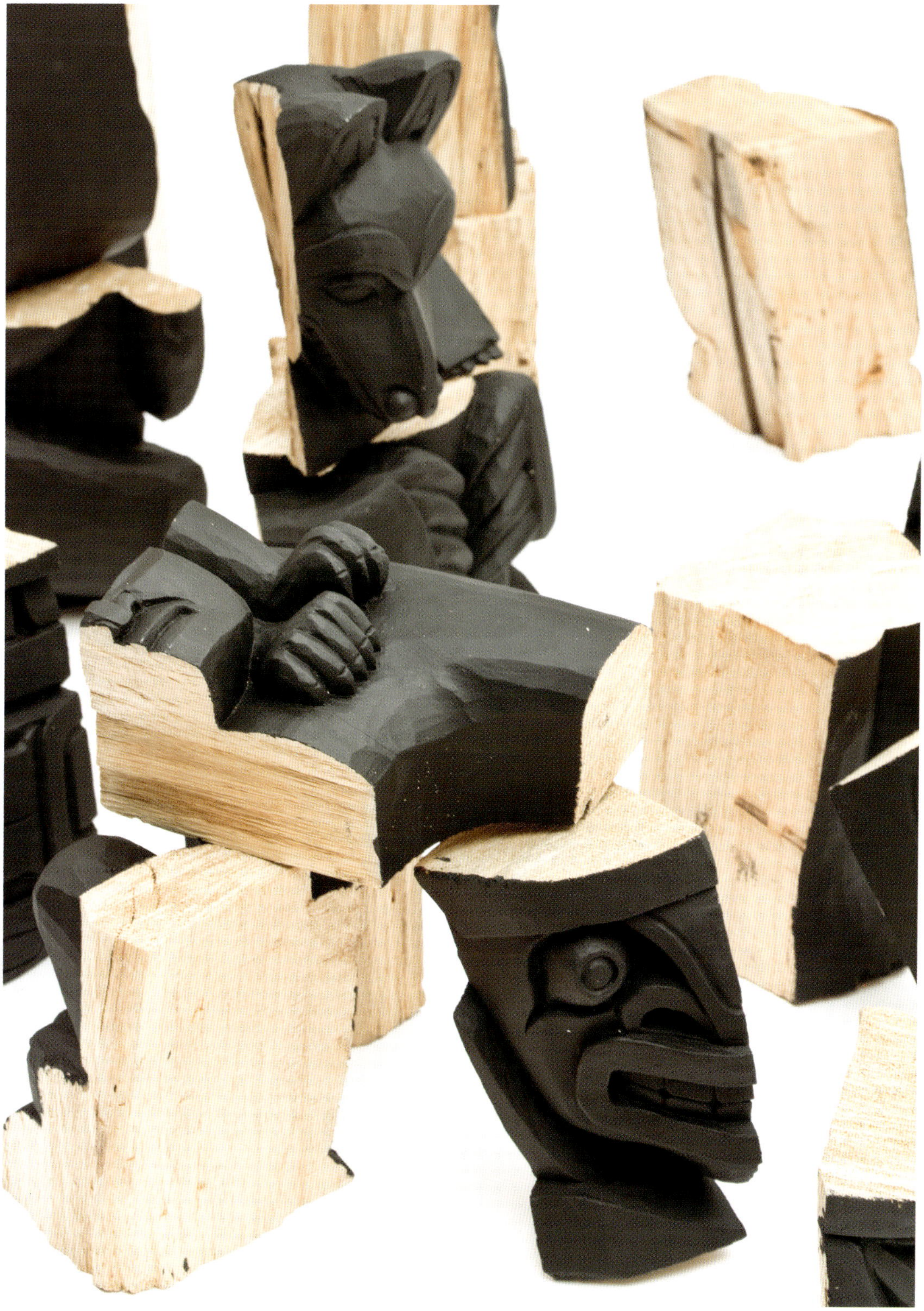

I Think It Goes Like This? (detail), 2012. Wood, paint.

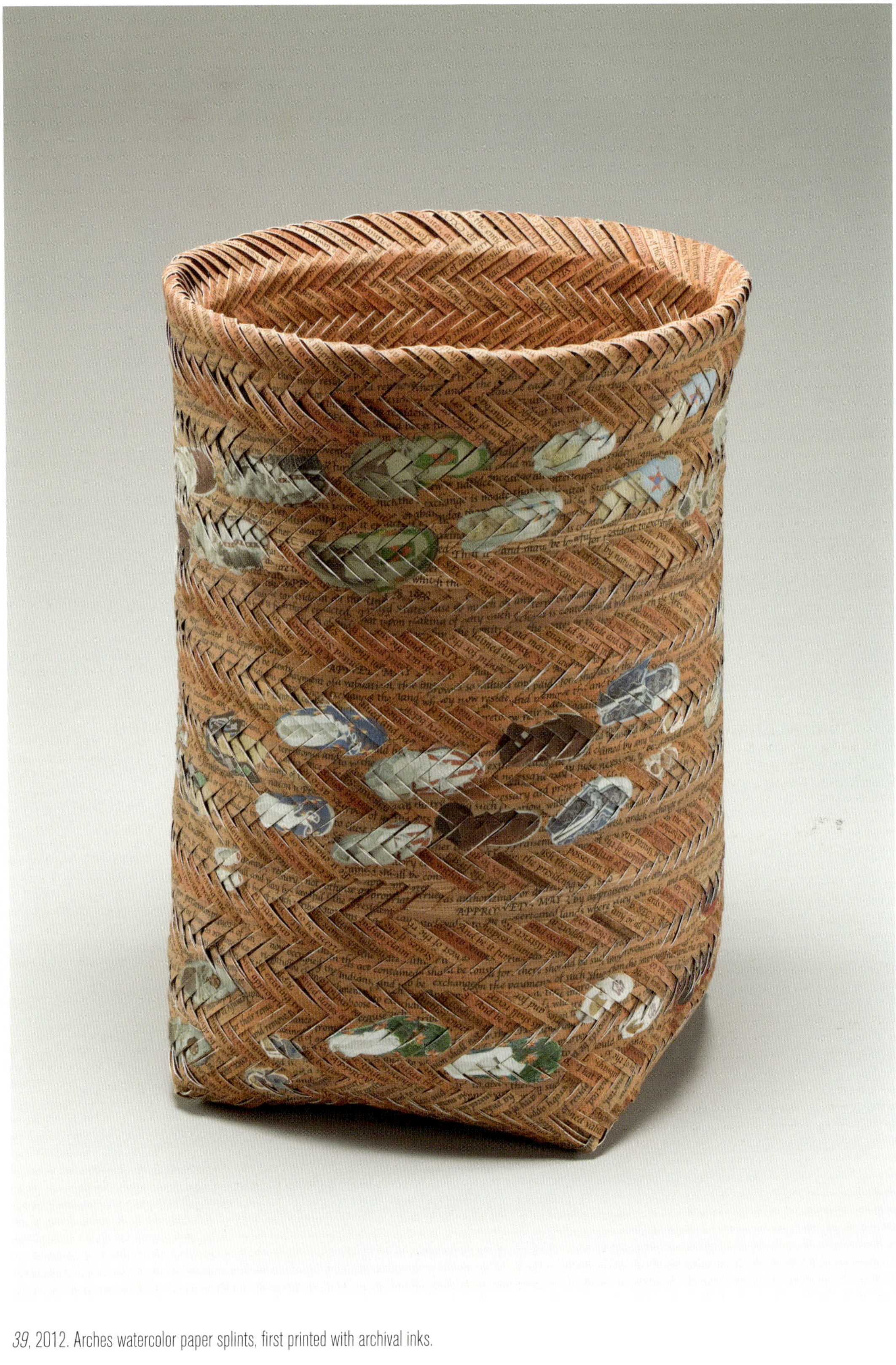

39, 2012. Arches watercolor paper splints, first printed with archival inks.

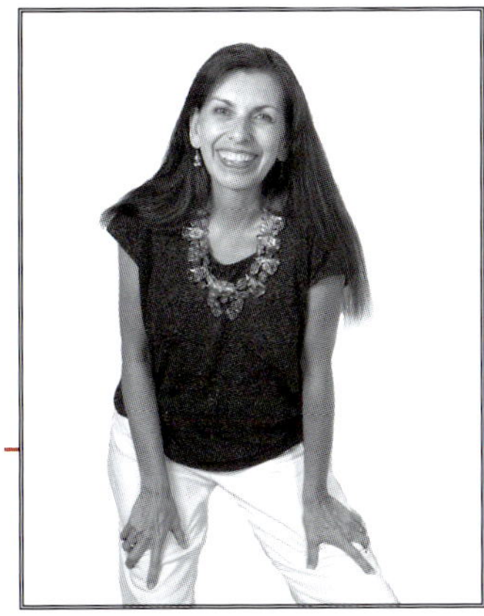

Shan Goshorn

(Eastern Band of Cherokee)

Leaning In to Shan Goshorn's Baskets

heather ahtone (Chickasaw and Choctaw Nations of Oklahoma)

I strive to educate an audience about some of the unique issues that continue to impact Indian people.

One of the most exciting developments in American Indian art this century has been the renaissance in basket making. Gail Tremblay, Shawna Cain, Jeremy Frey, and Sarah Sense are among those who have brought new vision to woven materials, invigorating the art form with fresh conceptual approaches similar to what happened to traditional pottery in the 1990s.[1] Native artists have taken the techniques and materials of a time-honored traditional form and breathed new life into a medium that had been relatively stagnant for over half a century. Since 2008, Shan Goshorn has become one of the most fearless weavers. Recognized nationally for her hand-painted photography and abstract paintings, Goshorn has always been a multi-media artist. By integrating her vision for photography and human rights activism into woven baskets, she has silently given voice to her culturally driven messages.

Goshorn lives in Tulsa, Oklahoma, and regularly travels home to North Carolina to connect with her extended family and her Eastern Band Cherokee community. As a full-time working artist, she credits working with the Qualla Arts & Crafts Mutual cooperative for giving her a broad knowledge of traditional Cherokee crafts. While working there as a teenager in college, Goshorn contracted with the Indian Arts and Crafts Board to prepare book illustrations of traditional basket designs. This job required her to look closely at how baskets are woven together. It seeded within her the desire to try weaving, but she never attempted the medium unti 2008, when she conceived the idea that a basket could serve as a metaphor of complex concepts related to traditional Native identity and contemporary issues. Her first conceptual basket addressed sovereignty, a metaphor expressing the interwoven and convoluted relationships between tribes and states. She employed the Tobacco Compact between the State of Oklahoma and the Cherokee Nation printed on paper as the material. Titled *Pieced Treaties; Spider's Web Treaty Basket*, the basket's technical success confirmed to her that she had found a new vessel for conveying her complex ideas.[2]

From this initial success was born *Educational Genocide—The Legacy of the Carlisle Indian Boarding School*.[3] She chose the coffin-shaped double-weave basket primarily because she was trying to challenge her ever-increasing weaving skill. Actually, she did not know the form was called a coffin until it was finished. It was constructed with a warp and weft made from a historical photo of American Indian children who had attended the Carlisle Indian School, combined with the text of Colonel Richard Henry Pratt's 1892 speech promoting cultural assimilation, from which the axiom "Save the Man, Kill the Indian" was born. The interior was constructed from a list of the names of the children who had attended the school. Goshorn described that she felt "intensely intimate.... I felt connected to those children."[4] Her attachment was amplified when she found the names of her relatives among those she was weaving. This solemn-shaped basket posits the children looking at the twenty-first century viewer as a metaphor for the innumerable lost childhoods, and even children, victims of the institutional boarding school system that created an ongoing legacy of historical trauma. This cultural legacy is, unfortunately, still festering over a century later in tribal communities in the form of endangered languages and lost cultural heritage. *Educational Genocide* was a pivotal piece for Goshorn. Through this basket, she connected with an audience broader than ever before, often emotionally, and viewers were eager to lean in on their own to try to understand what Goshorn was saying about the Native American subjects. The baskets are beautifully woven, but it is her choice of visual imagery combined with carefully selected texts and forms that makes them keen messengers.

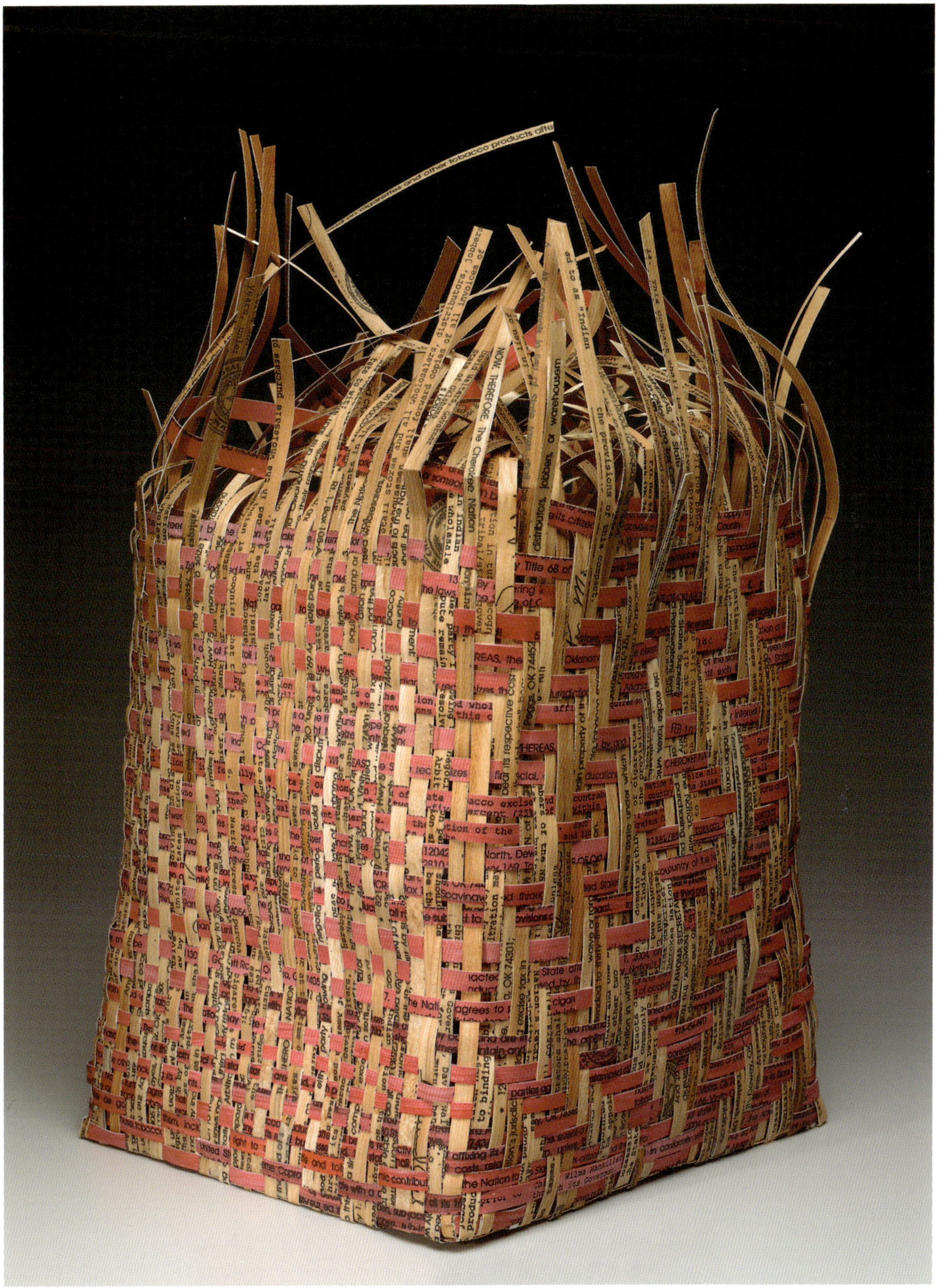

Pieced Treaties; Spider's Web Treaty Basket, 2008. Arches watercolor paper splints, first printed with archival inks. Image courtesy National Museum of the American Indian, Smithsonian Institution (266080.000). Photograph by Ernest Amoroso.

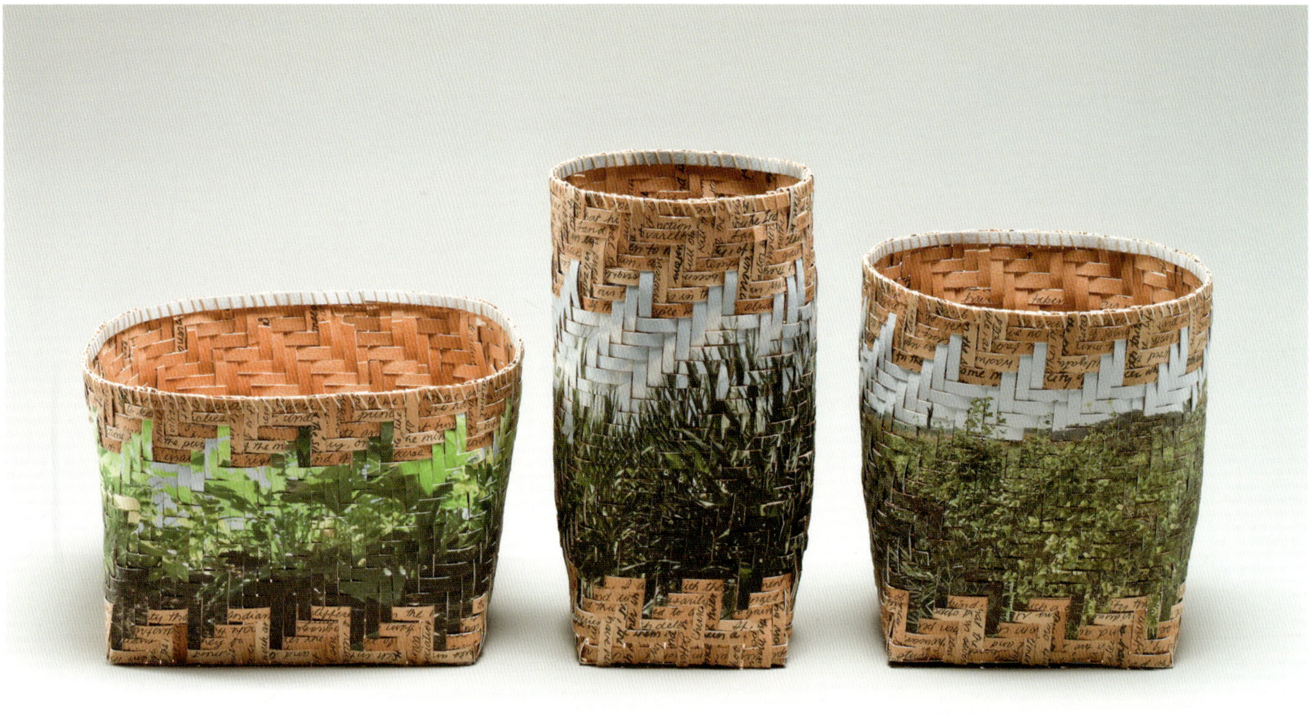

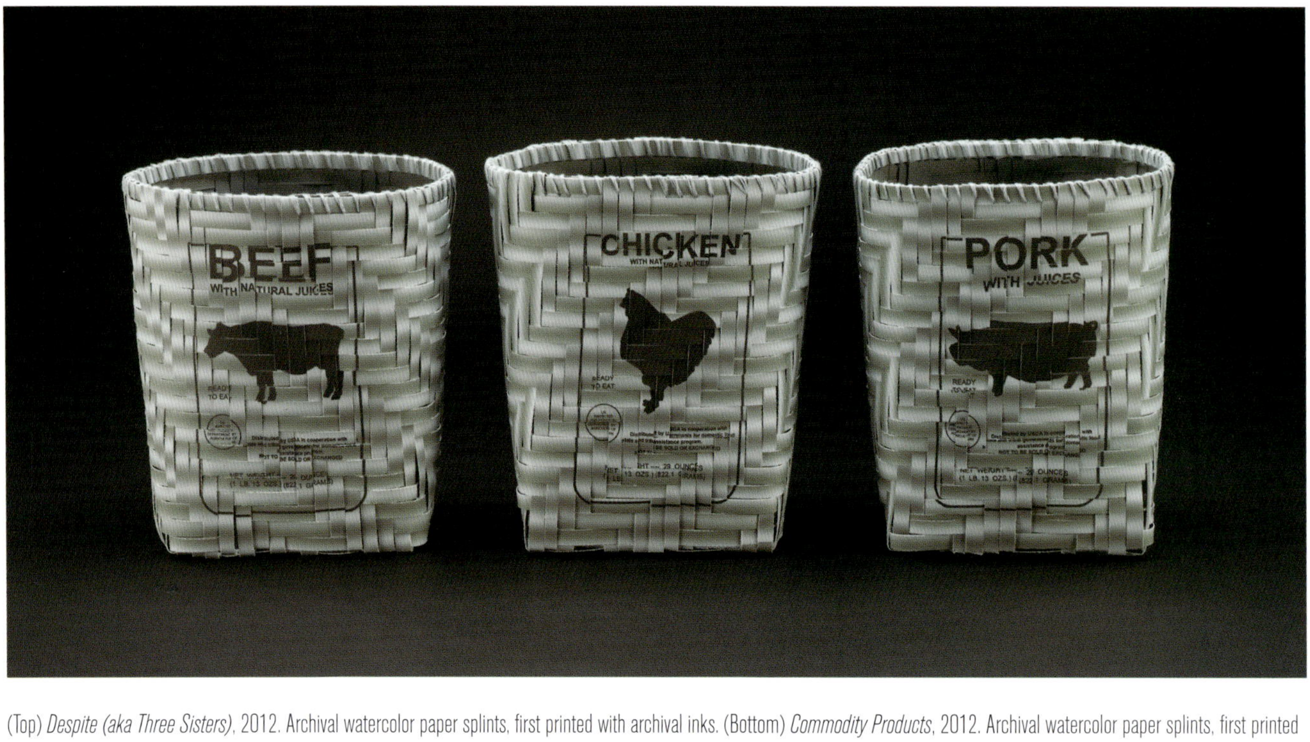

(Top) *Despite (aka Three Sisters)*, 2012. Archival watercolor paper splints, first printed with archival inks. (Bottom) *Commodity Products*, 2012. Archival watercolor paper splints, first printed with archival inks. Image courtesy of the Minneapolis Institute of Arts, The Patricia and Peter Frechette Endowment for Art Acquisition, 2013.11.1-.3.

Since making that connection, Goshorn has been exploring a range of subjects that work within this metaphorically potent medium. In 2012, she completed a set of nesting baskets called *Despite (aka Three Sisters)*. Goshorn wanted people to think about the multivalent symbolism of the three staples of the Cherokee diet, corn, beans, and squash, often called the "three sisters." She photographed the Cherokee community gardens near the Kituwah mound, going both figuratively and geographically to the Mother. These gardens, located at an ancestral homeland that has only recently been reacquired by the Cherokee community, serve to communicate the greater message that "despite the attempts at assimilation, we are still grounded within our traditional ways."[5] The subtitle refers to the symbiotic relationship of the plants that are traditionally grown in a companion intercropping system that is also called "Three Sisters."[6] The seeds are mound-planted with the corn in the middle, surrounded by the beans, which are surrounded by the squash. The corn provides the structure upon which the beans grow, and the beans reciprocate by providing the nitrogen to the soil that the corn needs. The squashes provide shade that limits weeds and prickly vines that deter animals from eating the more delicate beans and corn. The forms of the baskets follow the structure of the plants, with the basket woven from the photograph of corn standing taller and thinner within the shorter bean basket, within the wide and low-rimmed squash basket. The color photographic presence of the sky and the plants as an abundant crop were incorporated into each basket so that the relationship between the plants and the earth and the sky is incorporated into the body of the basket, which by its form becomes the human presence in the image.

Despite (aka Three Sisters) is a set of three, single woven baskets that visually reference all that Kituwah represents. An ancestral land of the Cherokee, founded as one of the "seven mother towns" as early as 1000 CE, it was lost during Andrew Jackson's reign of terror. Ceded during treaty negotiations, the land was privately held from the mid-1830s until the cusp of the twenty-first century, when it was bought back by the tribe for communal use. The tribe's reconnection with the land is partnered with the return to the traditional food staples. Because obesity and diabetes have plagued tribal communities, the latter having been deemed an epidemic by the Centers for Disease Control and Prevention, many communities are adamantly working to return to their traditional foodways.[7] These reconnections to traditional culture and practices are strengthening not only their identity but also improving their overall health and well-being. The baskets speak to the relationship that the Cherokee have to the homeland, rooted through their culture, to a place. Furthermore, Native people find personal harmony through their culture, through the practice of the tribal language and rituals, nurtured through reciprocity with the extended community. These extensions into the natural environment are critical to the philosophy of the tribe and reflect how they understand the world. The plants are called "three sisters" because the Cherokee people believe they have a direct relationship with these plants, far beyond the obvious food source. Goshorn explained that the title is a direct commentary to this philosophical tenet: "It is because despite the efforts to assimilate Native children, we remain rooted in our ancient ways."[8]

Goshorn speaks to the relationship that exists between health, tribal land, culture, and traditions through these delicate baskets. Perhaps it is the delicacy of the beautiful imagery, anchored by impeccable craftsmanship, that makes the baskets such a powerful expression of the issues Goshorn is raising. She has been speaking to audiences and through her art on these topics for years, but she observed that there was too little dialogue taking place. Her audience had previously only listened, the issues were too stark, and the challenges so great that people had previously politely disconnected. But now Goshorn sees them leaning in to engage, asking more questions and eager to learn about the subjects presented. Goshorn said, "My art has become a springboard for honest discussion to happen right now."[9] She believes the ancestors are supporting her as she pushes forward to bring these topics to bear within the baskets. Through the carefully balanced weave of these pliable materials, photographs and speeches printed on pressed wood and cotton pulp, archival inks, the delicate nature of a basket—these have become Goshorn's weapons of cultural warfare.

Careful to select the subject for each work, Goshorn presented the issue of tribal relationship to land from a slightly different perspective in the basket titled *39*. Goshorn solicited her friends across Oklahoma to share their moccasins through photography. She avoided the archival references of historic photos because it was important to her that the image conveyed how traditional materials are still tied to living cultures. This aspect was conceptually integrated into the soliciting process. These photographs were often provided digitally, emailed to Goshorn's Internet account. Thereby the "moccasin trail" was transformed digitally via the World Wide Web. Goshorn wove the photographs on the diagonal proscribed by the double-weave basket form, very similar to traditional gathering or storage baskets. The images of the moccasins were bound together with the Indian Removal Act of 1830, which is visible on the interior and exterior between the rows of moccasins pairs. This historic document, printed on brownish-toned paper to make it look wooden, gave Andrew Jackson the power to negotiate with tribes for western removal, although he used it as a premise to forcibly remove tribes from their traditional homelands into Indian Territory. The title is a reference to the thirty-nine pairs of moccasins on the basket. It is also a reference to the thirty-nine federally recognized tribes that call Oklahoma home, many of whom entered the territory during the Removal Era.

This double-walled basket was started from the interior bottom, woven on a diagonal to the desired height when the walls were turned down to finish at the bottom. The image and text were necessarily cut so that they could be woven into one another without losing the identity of the subjects as the weaving was turned down. Around the exterior of the basket are thirty-nine pairs of moccasins, contemporary and inter-tribal, forming a ribbon that rotates from the upper rim down to the bottom. The visual path they form around the vessel expresses those migrations that take place on a regular basis, going between the ceremonial communities—more often than not still bound to particular sacred sites—and the often-urban homes where Native people participate in American society with jobs and schools in a manner that is every bit as contemporary as that of their neighbors. These migrations might be seen as the contemporary extension of the seasonal migrations that historically created a broad continental trade network, or even the forced march that many ancestors made almost two centuries ago.

It is a reality that Oklahoma has become a hub for Indian Country, continuing to be one of the most culturally diverse states in the union. That diverse Native population is very much a reflection of the federal policy that brought tribes as different as the Modoc from California and the Wyandotte from Canada and the Seminole from Florida into the shared space of Oklahoma. Goshorn herself represents the further Native diversity that is found in Oklahoma: those Native people who have found their way to the state and call it "home," although their tribal communities are elsewhere. For these people, the Native community of Oklahoma is often another family, establishing roots with the tribes here and participating in the local fellowship while still making migrations to participate in their own tribal ceremonies. This is evident on the basket in the visibly different moccasins from the Navajo and Pueblo communities of the Southwest, as well as beaded designs from the Lakota and Ojibwe. The reality is that there are more than just thirty-nine tribes represented in Oklahoma. These tribal people physically manifest the connections to places across the continent, no less dynamic than the Internet that brought their images to Goshorn for the basket.

The form of the basket, used for gathering, serves as a metaphor for the lived reality of that historic document. The basket can be seen as a metaphor for the state of Oklahoma, a gathering place for Native people. Perhaps what is most strongly represented by the basket's rigid form is that many tribes have held onto their traditional arts and that these remain available for young artists to pick up and connect with their cultures. That mix of tradition and contemporaneity, especially through the vitality of culture and art, Goshorn says, "is so satisfying."

The aspect of the baskets that is perhaps most poignant, critical to their metaphorical currency, is found in the preparation process. Goshorn's thoughtfully selected visual material, often a historic text document and a photographic image, must be prepared and scaled for printing in a final size that suits the intended form. It takes multiple prints of the primary source, each meticulously cut to an exact width and length in both vertical and horizontal strips, if not diagonal strips, from which Goshorn will then begin the weaving process. It is in the cutting, this physical deconstruction of history—both text and image, the slicing and dissecting—that the metaphor takes root. For many tribes, paper has been used as a weapon against their cultures, their sovereignty, and their identities. Goshorn takes the pieces she has broken down and reconstructs them into baskets. These forms, all built following traditions that reach farther back than federal history, speak to the continuum that lives within the cultures, the legacies that breathe in each new generation of Native artists, ready to be picked up and carried through the twenty-first century by the young people Goshorn is inspiring with her art.

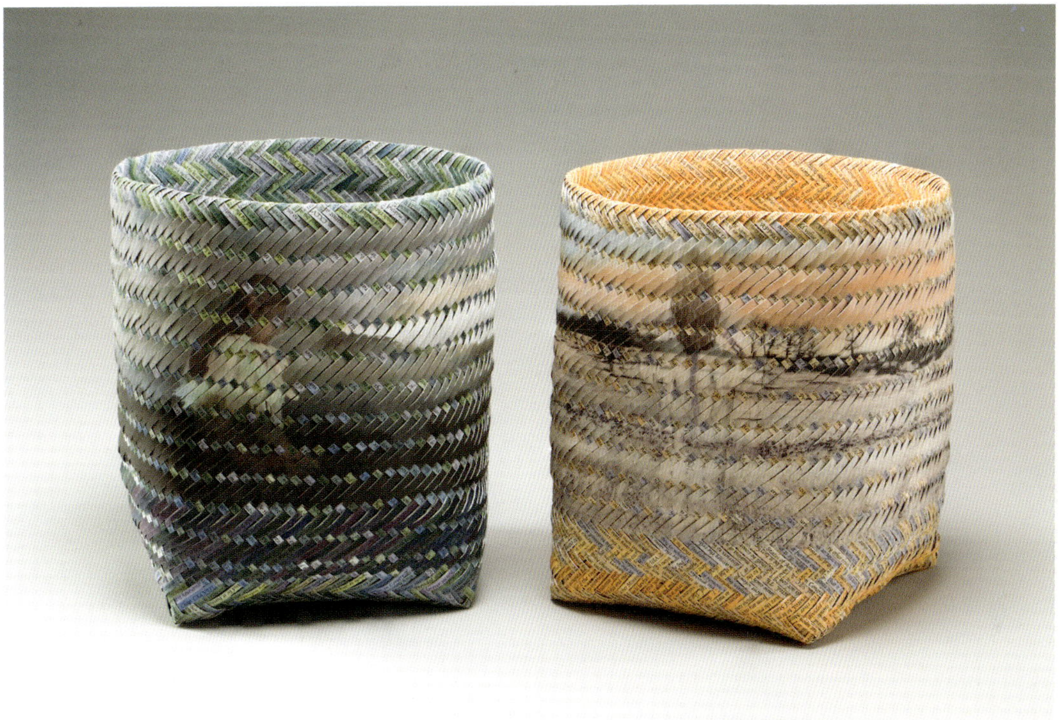

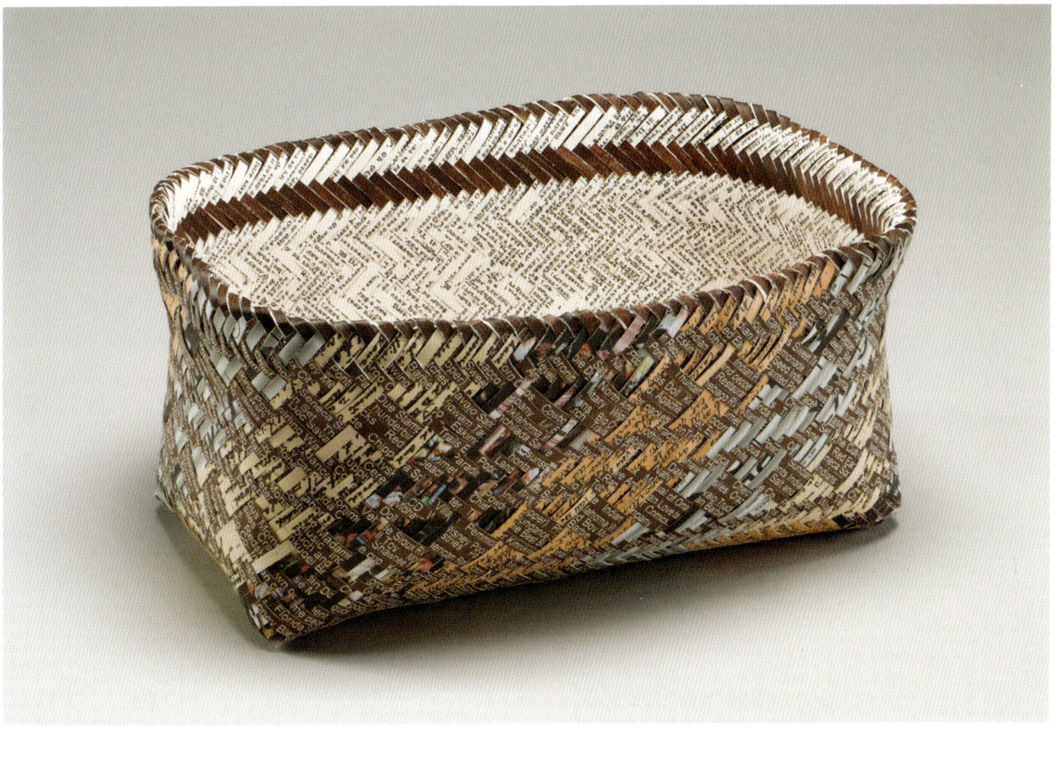

(Above left) *Removal (Ancestral Homeland)* and (right) *Removal (Indian Territory)*, 2012. Mixed media. (Below) *Unsolicited Gifts or How to Eliminate a Culture*, 2012. Archival watercolor paper splints, first printed with archival inks.

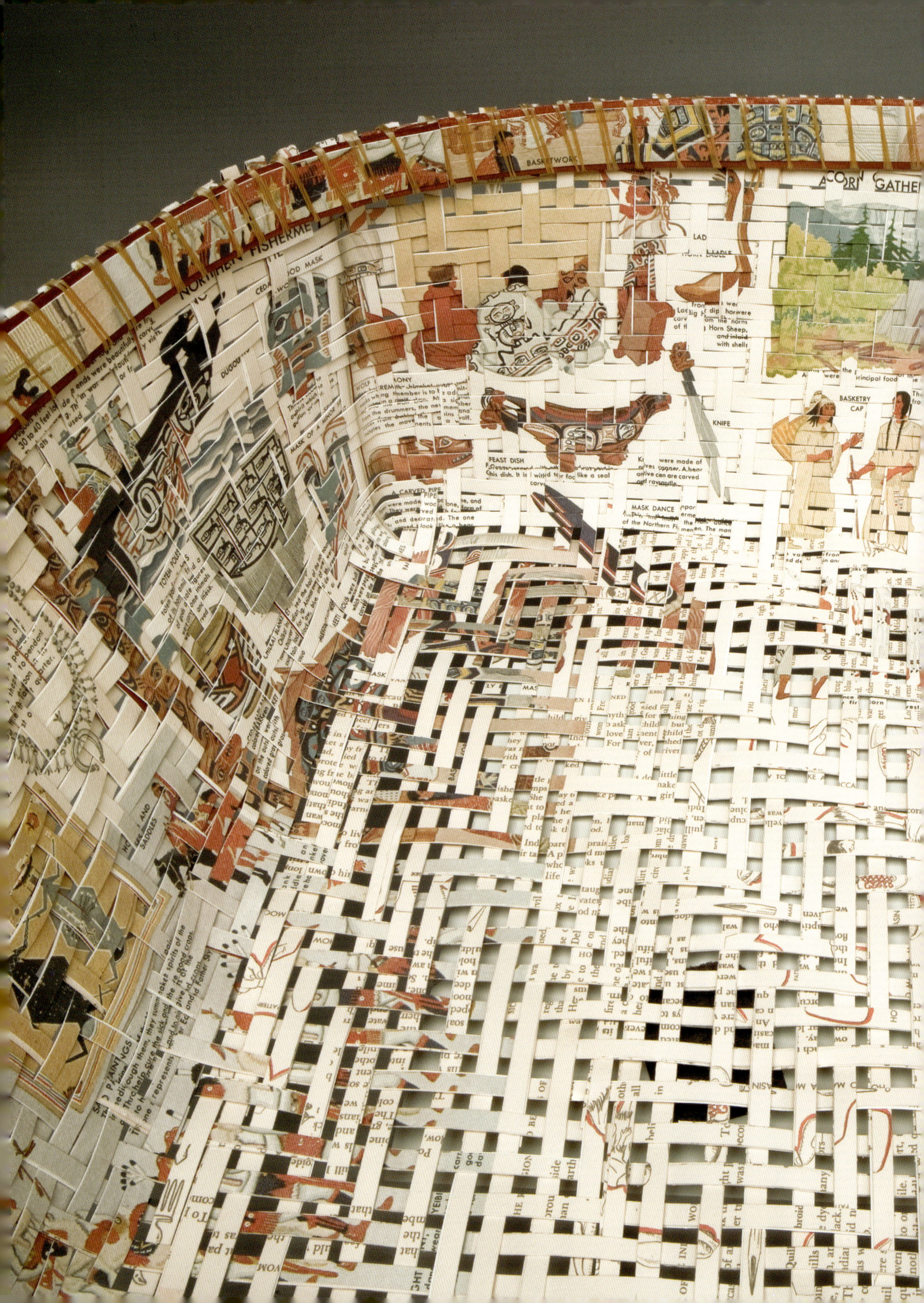

The nature of that process is part of their temporality. They could not have been constructed with these same methods before now.

In no other basket is that deconstruction more critical than in *Separating the Chaff*, a sifter or winnowing basket constructed from images borrowed from reference books that date to the 1960s. These books were similar to the very ones Goshorn had been taught out of as a primary student in the same era. "Some of the information is true. Some of the information is just so cheesy it will curl your hair," Goshorn said. "It occurred to me that the information being taught in schools today is not really that much different now, as I watch my kids go through school." There is so much information about American Indian cultures that provide broad generalizations, often making the error of speaking of the race as if it is a set of regional groups. "There was a page for the Northwest Coast Indians, a page for the Plains Indians. Everyone gets kind of lumped together." These kinds of instructional texts often leave American students with more misinformation than knowledge. As Native people, Goshorn says, "we need to filter through the information that is being taught and accept responsibility to proactively teach about ourselves."[10]

Goshorn was challenged to create a sifter basket with the strength to hold its shape despite being made out of material as soft as paper. As she initially wove the basket, a process she undertook three times before it was completed, the walls could not hold the weight of the structure. That has its own metaphorical interpretation, as though the information itself did not provide enough strength from which to work. But she saw that "some of the information was really correct, but let's get it in context and get rid of what is not."[11] Goshorn worked to reinforce the walls, adding layers from the same pages woven into the sides and an additional rim support attached with synthetic sinew. Goshorn had a feeling it would work, and so, despite the initial weakness, she endeavored to reinforce the information with layers of more imagery and more text, working with what she could find to provide the strength to hold the traditional form in place. She manifestly took responsibility for making that information work as a resource material. The illustrations and text have been woven back together into a basket that reminds us that we each have a responsibility to sift through the "chaff" of misinformation and seek out the kernels of truth.

(Left) *Separating the Chaff* (detail), 2013. Archival watercolor paper splints, first printed with archival inks.

The success of *Separating the Chaff* might be seeded in that commitment to set creative challenges and to see the object through to its greatest potential.[12] Goshorn recognizes that her intuitive creativity often produces art that is even better than her original intention. This can be seen in her choice of color for the exterior, a burnt red or sienna that resonated for her as "blood, stop, boldness, action, agitation."[13] She primarily chose red because she wanted it to work cohesively with the colors of the content illustration. Many of the early illustrations commonly have red in their palette. Goshorn's selection of red as an exterior color reminds the viewer of the consequences of ignorance, visually invoking racial slurs that have been used against American Indians: the "redskin" and "red man." While Goshorn did not intend the slurs specifically, she embraces the notion that these layers of meaning can be read into the work. Even when she finishes a piece, the connection viewers make to the art reveals other interpretations that are equally powerful and valid to her. These stories and responses become part of the life of the art.

The deconstruction process that Goshorn uses to create the source materials, which she then weaves back into the traditional basket forms, effectively debunks the historicizing effect sometimes found in working in traditional, cultural arts. She expresses a deep affection for the artists who have kept these traditional art forms alive, seeing her work an extension of that continuum.

It is not enough, though, for Goshorn to simply make traditional baskets. That is what makes her work so exciting. These baskets are following traditions and would not be the same without the traditions, but they are fully of the present, dependent on the Internet and contemporary printing techniques. Using historical images and texts, but bringing the kind of hindsight and critical review that only the passing of time makes possible, Goshorn creates an object that evokes thoughtful dialogue about issues that matter to contemporary audiences. These baskets speak to the contemporary identity of Goshorn as a traditional person within her Cherokee culture. They speak to federal policy, culture, the earth, and racial politics. Because of their exquisite craftsmanship, these daunting topics are made accessible. The dialogue, like the baskets themselves, has become constructive.

Most powerfully, the baskets speak to viewers whose emotional responses have triggered the kind of dialogue that Goshorn could only dream of through her earlier work as an activist. The response people have to the baskets has contributed to national recognition for the artist and earned her multiple awards and fellowships. For Goshorn, the baskets feed her intellectual and artistic appetite. She recognizes that the baskets are creating an audience for the issues, an audience she is only just recently beginning to gauge. The success she has experienced through the baskets has not interrupted her work as a photographer and other business endeavors, but she plans to continue working in baskets as long as they resonate for her. Reflecting on the timelessness of these basket forms and the critical discussion they are inspiring, truly, the ancestors must be smiling.

---

[1]These indigenous artists represent diverse tribal basket traditions: Gail Tremblay is Onondaga and Mi'kmaq, Shawna Cain is Cherokee, Jeremy Frey is Passamaquoddy, and Sarah Sense is Chitimacha and Choctaw.

[2]*Pieced Treaties: Spider's Web Treaty Basket* was purchased by the National Museum of the American Indian, Smithsonian Institution, Washington, D.C.

[3]*Educational Genocide* is currently traveling in the exhibition *Changing Hands: Art Without Reservation 3, Contemporary Native North American Art from the Northeast and Southeast,* organized by the Museum of Arts and Design (MAD) and curated by guest curator Ellen Taubman in collaboration with MAD's Chief Curator David McFadden, New York City.

[4]Personal communication with author, June 7, 2013.

[5]Ibid.

[6]"Three Sisters" is the term used by the Cherokee and other Southeastern Native American tribes to refer to the companion plants of corn, beans, and squash. The term has been adopted by agriculturalists to refer to both the plants and/or the system.

[7] "Fact Sheet: Trends in Diabetes Prevalence among American Indian and Alaska Native Children, Adolescents, and Young Adults—1990–1998," National Center for Chronic Disease Prevention and Health Promotion, Division of Diabetes Translation, 2011.

[8]Personal communication with author, June 25, 2013.

[9]Personal communication with author, June 7, 2013.

[10]Ibid.

[11]Ibid.

[12]*Separating the Chaff* was finished just prior to the 2013 Annual Heard Market. At its debut, Goshorn received awards for best of class in baskets, first place in non-traditional baskets, and a judge's choice award. At that market, noted collector James T. Bialac purchased the basket to add to his Native American art collection at the Fred Jones Jr. Museum of Art, University of Oklahoma.

[13]Personal communication with author, June 25, 2013.

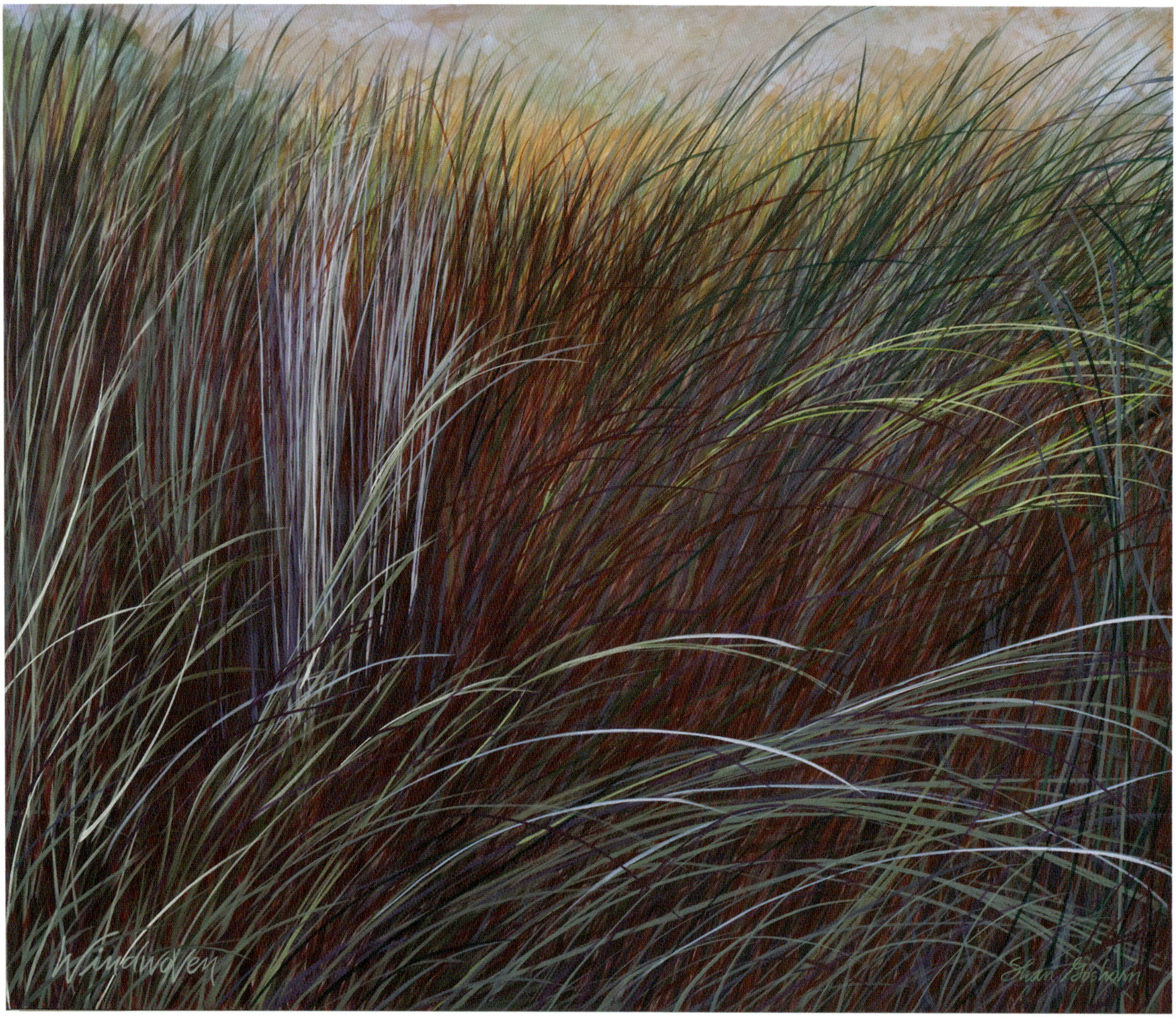

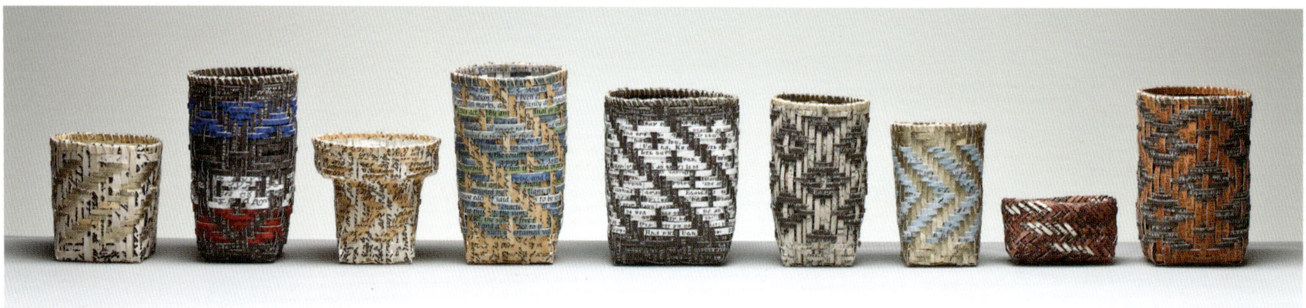

(Above) *Windwoven*, 2013. Acrylic on canvas. (Below, left to right) nine miniature baskets (*Gold Exchanged; Theological Discussion; On the Shoulders of a Child; Turned a Blind Eye; It's Not Just Black and White; Double Crossed; Golden Rule, Overruled; Forever a Part of Us; Underhanded Allies*), 2012–2013. Mixed media.

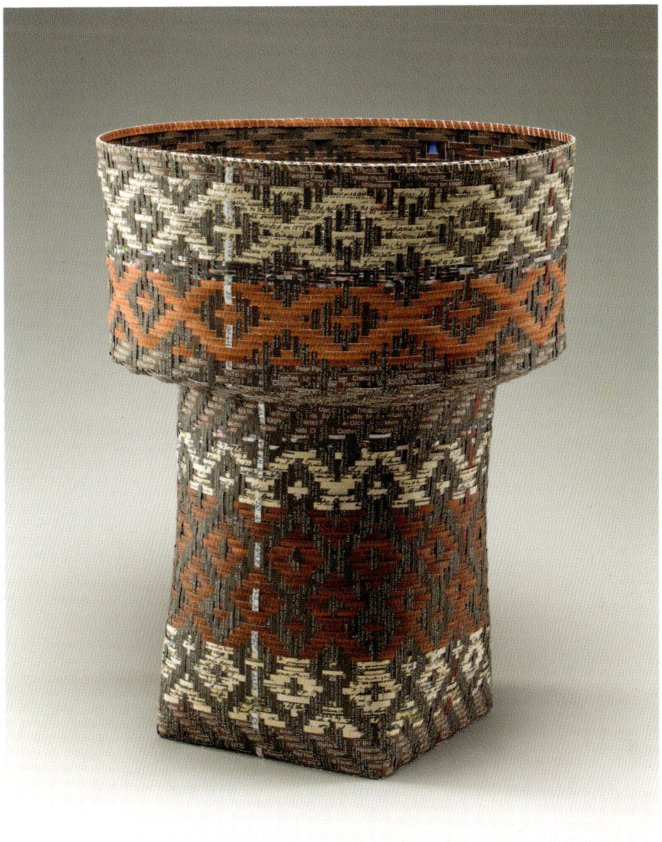

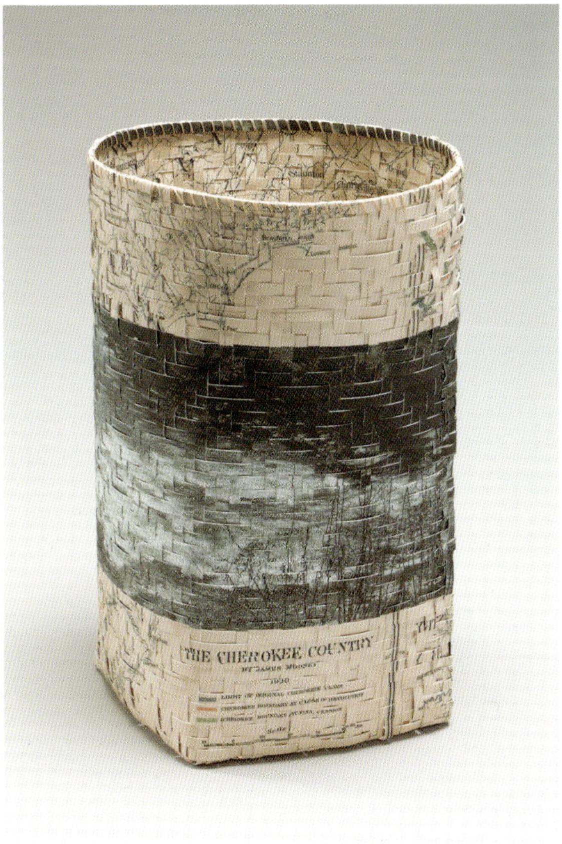

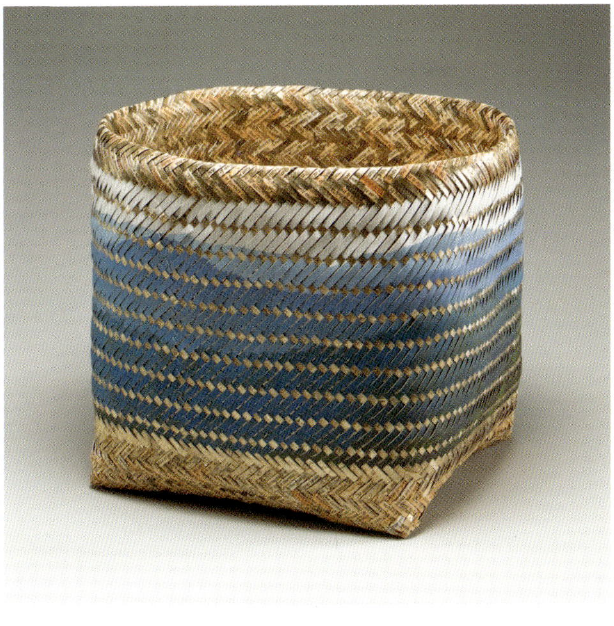

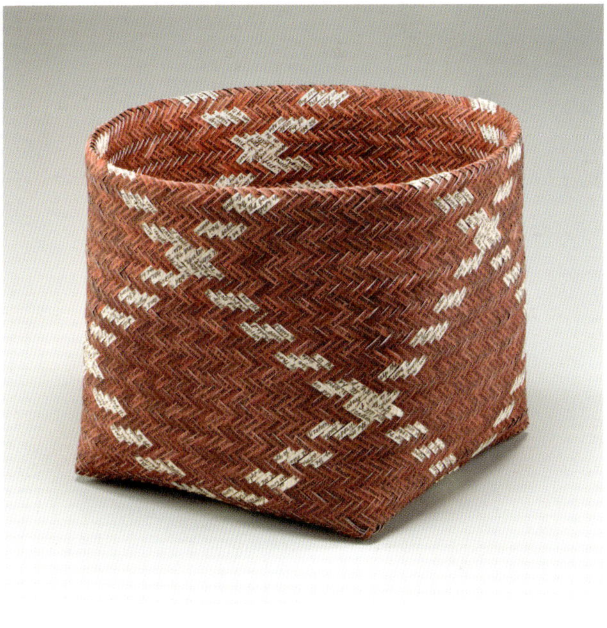

(Above left) *Cherokee Burden Basket; Singing a Song for Balance*, 2013. Archival watercolor paper splints, first printed with archival inks. (Above right) *So Long as These Waters Run*, 2012. Arches watercolor paper splints, first printed with archival inks. (Below left) *All They Could See in Blue Mountains Was Gold*, 2012. Mixed media.(Bottom right) *Forever Woven into Our Fabric*, 2012. Archival watercolor paper splints, first printed with archival inks.

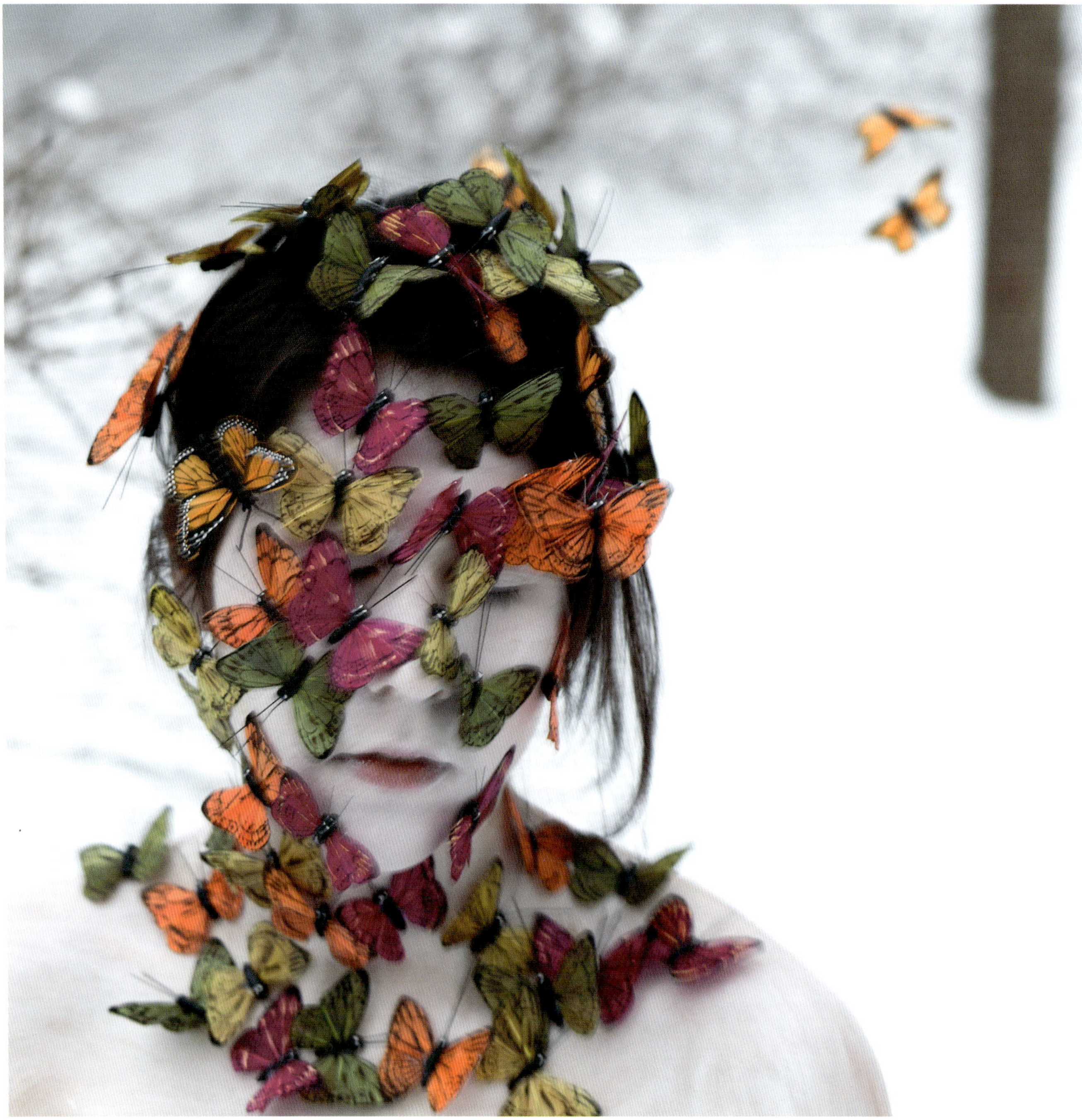

Anima (In-Between Worlds series*)*, 2012. Digital chromogenic print. Image courtesy the artist.

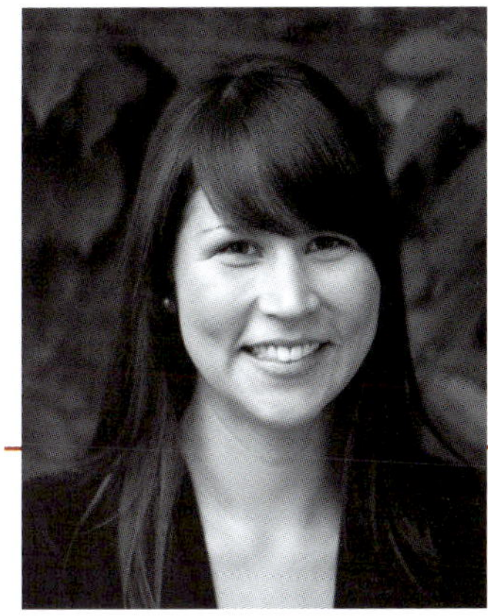

Meryl McMaster

(Plains Cree/Blackfoot)

Immeasurable, the Art of Being

Ashley Holland (Cherokee)[1]

My artistic practice begins with photography evoking a journey that follows a path of self-discovery.... My art unravels notions of identity and subjectivity as something that is never complete, but always in process and always formed from within.

Meryl McMaster's work creates a paradigm of the artist as visual philosopher. Her pursuit of knowledge, connection to the natural world, and relentless dedication to profound beauty make her photographs sumptuous and complex. They are a world unto themselves. She invites the viewers to join her in this world, to take what they may, and to grow from their own conclusions.

McMaster was born to a Euro-Canadian mother and Plains Cree/Blackfoot father in 1988. Her father, Gerald McMaster, is a well-known artist, author, and curator of Canadian aboriginal contemporary art. There is little question that this upbringing gave McMaster a great well of cultural and ancestral memory in which to immerse and emerge as herself. It is also of no small consequence that she, as an early career artist, exists in the era of important cultural and social movements such as Idle No More, in which Canada's aboriginal people strive to reclaim their place and rights in their communities locally, provincially, and nationally.[2] No doubt this influences her political and social views, of which her photographs act as a visual record.

A graduate of Ontario College of Art and Design (OCAD) in Toronto, McMaster received her bachelor of fine arts degree in photography. While at OCAD, she approached her work through personal reinterpretations of the philosophical, artistic, and cultural influences she encountered. In all McMaster is exposed to, she absorbs knowledge and experiences and creates imagery that is uniquely hers. In her senior thesis, she talked extensively about the search for self-discovery and identity.

Searching for life meaning led me to discover the idea of the quest in the work of French anthropologist Arnold Van Gennep and his work on the "rites of passage." Whether it was camping or struggling through university, I found historical equivalents in the ancient practice of the vision quest. The vision quest is not always about finding visions but a search for meaning and the consequence of struggling with others or with oneself. The vision quest was seen as a rite of passage. Van Gennep describes it as an once-in-a-lifetime experience in which boys become men and girls become women. This usually began with an individual's physical removal from the community, in which they would be set out in nature, alone, for a period of time. This being alone Van Gennep describes is a "liminal" period.[3]

In her thesis, she went on to discuss British cultural anthropologist Victor Turner and his views on liminality: "Liminal entities are neither here nor there; they are betwixt and between the positions assigned and arrayed by law, custom, convention, and ceremonial."[4] It is this liminal state that McMaster would descend into to search for artistic inspiration, in sites in and around Toronto, often to places that other Native people had historically gone for leisure time.[5] And it was out of this state that she created her earlier works, which showed a depth and maturity beyond those of most young artists.

McMaster conceptualizes her work and then proceeds to use the moment, the environment, and the circumstance of that particular sequence to document the culmination of her vision. She has a space in her home where elements and concepts are envisioned and created as the stepping-stones to the act of photographing. For McMaster, the camera becomes an object that is vulnerable and dependent on the environment around it.[6] She takes cues from other artists such as Ann Hamilton and fellow OCAD graduate Rebecca Belmore (Anishinaabe). Hamilton's approach to installation and her use of texture and objects in space were particularly inspiring to McMaster. This building of the objects or sculptures that appear in the photographs is an important aspect of both Hamilton's and McMaster's process. Hamilton also often includes herself in the photograph. This is also seen in the work of Belmore, who focuses on the personal process of the performance. The idea that Belmore's "body became the cipher" appealed to McMaster and has affected how she approaches her own work.

Thus, I began inserting my own body into a visual space, to consider it sculpture as time, at the same time reflecting on my own bi-cultural memory. As I progressed, I began creating things that became not only props but also sculptures in themselves. My identity and history is written on my body. I do not see the kind of struggles that some see or experience; rather, I want to be able to see the possibilities that come with being bi-cultural.[7]

McMaster's photographs continue to grow stronger as she adds layer upon layer of experience toward the spiritual maturity she seeks. Her constant exploration of identity and search for (self) realization translate beautifully into lush images with each subject she captures. Her photography series *In-Between Worlds*, *Ancestral*, and *Second Self* demonstrate the potency of her artistic message. It is not surprising that one so interested in pursuit of the elevation of the human spirit and self-consciousness about her bi-cultural heritage would choose to work in the form of a photographic series, as if to better investigate a world, a view, through a multi-dimensional lens and a plethora of sculptural, cultural, and natural materials.

The *In-Between Worlds* series is McMaster's most varied and complex work in which she examines and expresses her bi-cultural heritage. McMaster does not view this dual identity as problematic, but rather as a part of who she is that constantly informs her way of thinking.[8] She is strategic in her thought process, and this calm is expressed through the visual narrative. As she notes, *In Between Worlds*, *can have moments that may appear out of the ordinary, since during the quest odd and unexplainable situations can occur. This was the beauty of this project in that it allowed me to experiment with various ideas. Therefore, these moments could be interpreted as being in a state of suspended belief; in other words, what you see is somewhat unbelievable and can only be considered being in an ethereal or otherworldly state.*[9]

The *In-Between Worlds* series encompasses over a dozen images, saturated with color and texture. The images are multi-dimensional in their visual and psychological presentation. McMaster is the subject, yet each photograph is a manifestation of the layers of experiences her life embodies. Each photograph depicts a different scene, full of a densely created narrative with sculpture and specific placement. In works such as *Horse Dance*, *Wingeds Calling*, and *Sentinence*, McMaster disappears seamlessly into the work, while in *Terra Cognitum*, *Aphoristic Currents*, and *Anima*, the artist is central. Even McMaster's eye contact with the viewer varies within the series. Works such as *Wind Play* and *Caduceus* remove the eyes all together. Averted gazes are featured in *Viage* and *Telltales*. Even when eye contact is made, only one eye is seen, as in *Tilsam* and *Victoria*. The varying degrees of gaze, subject, and the sequence of moments that appear out of the ordinary are McMaster's way of challenging viewers to question themselves and the world around them. They also demonstrate the way self-identity changes over time.

Through the series, McMaster investigates the nature of being and transforming of her identity. She creates a sequence of moments that depicts herself, nature, talismans, and sculptures as part of that world. Many of the sculptures featured within the works are objects McMaster found while out in nature, on her quests. In the *In-Between Worlds* series, she delves into ideas of New Materialism, a philosophy born from the examination of consumerism and the financial crises of recent times. It is a belief that objects hold energy; the better an object is crafted, the better the object is. New Materialism states that the "new new" is second-hand, repaired, or repurposed, and is the desired object. This attitude is reflected in *Caduceus*. In this work, McMaster has repurposed an umbrella. The shredded and fringed tartan

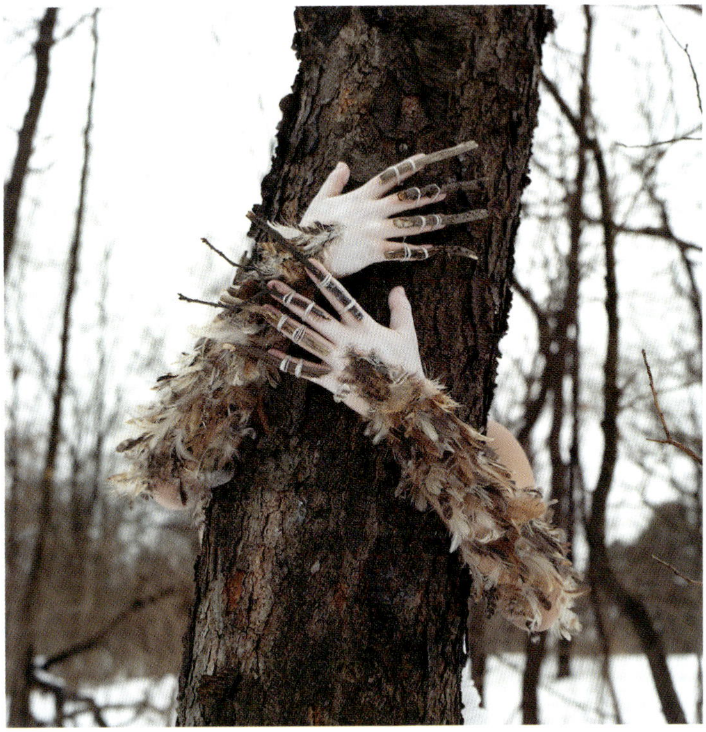

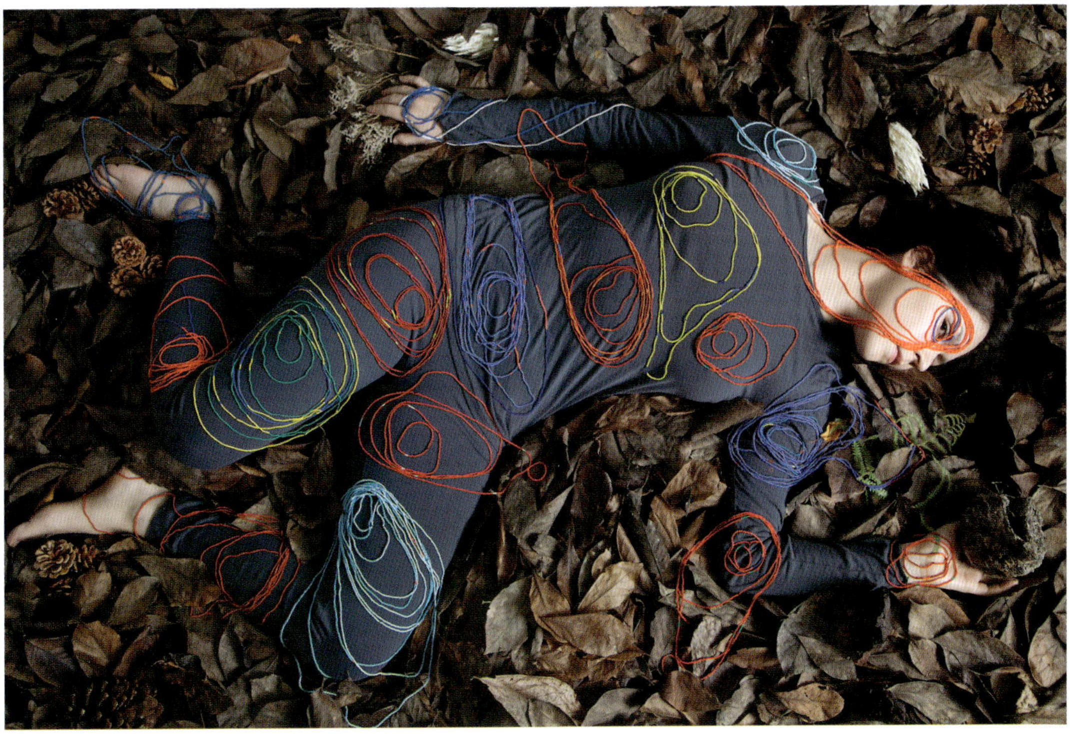

(Above) *Sentience (In-Between Worlds* series*)*, 2010. Digital chromogenic print. Image courtesy the artist. (Below) *Terra Cognitum (In-Between Worlds* series*)*, 2013. Digital chromogenic print. Image courtesy the artist.

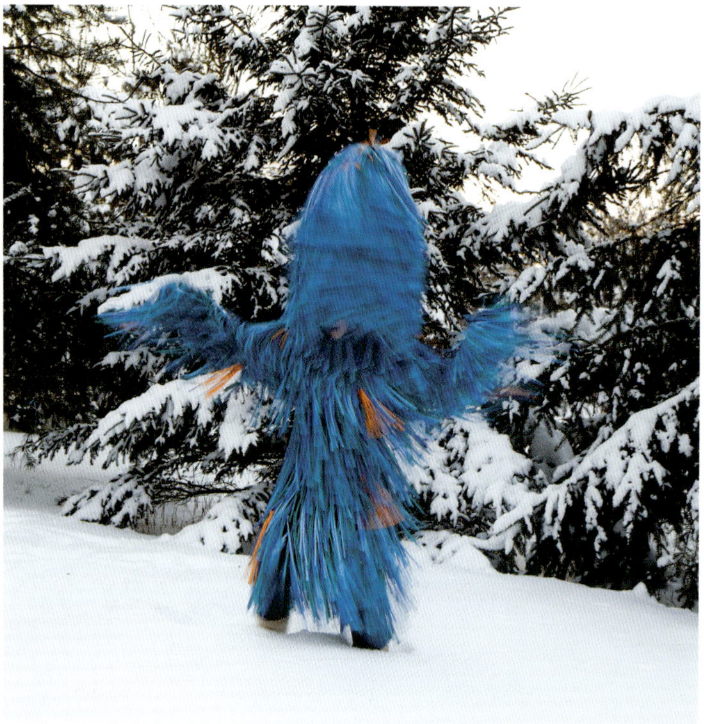

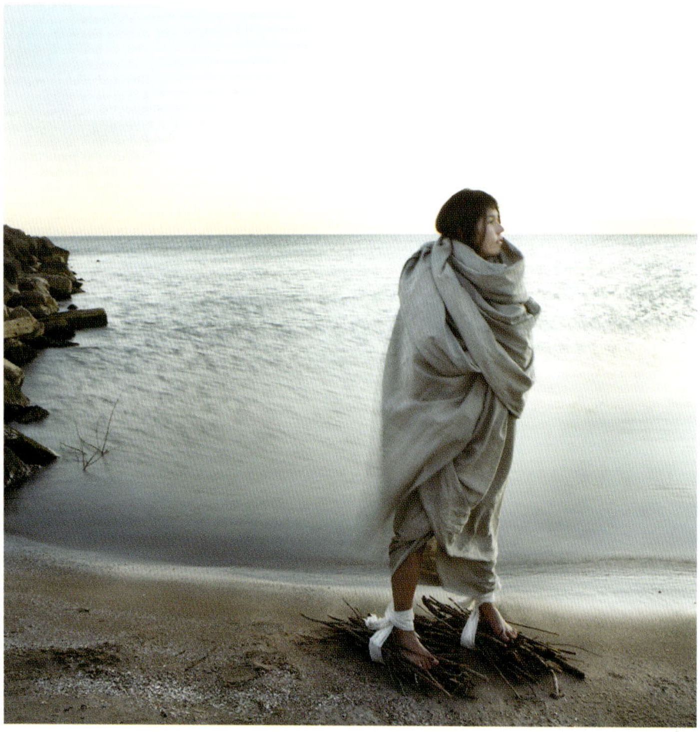

(Above) *Wind Play (In-Between Worlds* series*)*, 2012. Digital chromogenic print. Image courtesy the artist. (Below) *Viage (In-Between Worlds* series*)*, 2010. Digital chromogenic print. Image courtesy the artist.

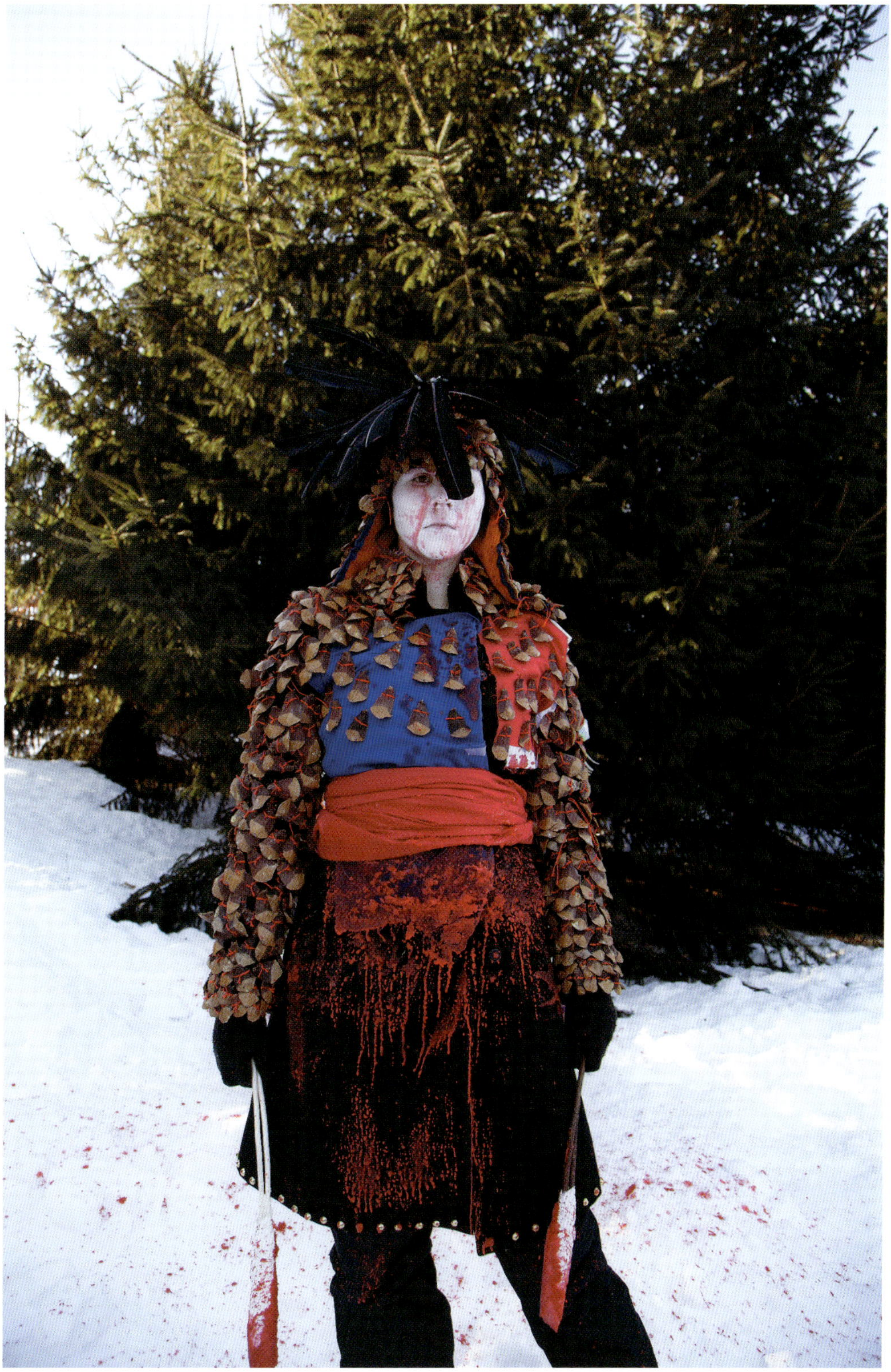

Victoria (In-Between Worlds series*)*, 2013. Digital chromogenic print. Image courtesy the artist.

print and weaving of twigs refer to her dual heritage, which she supports by holding the large, multi-faceted sculpture.[10]

Wingeds Calling goes further into the discussion of dual heritage. A cloaked raven stands on the shore of a body of water. The white fog descends on the white setting and contrasts with the black bird figure, which is covered with smaller birds and adorned by feathers with red and white decorations. The raven has multiple meanings—a trickster, wisdom keeper, and messenger—and is found in both European and aboriginal cultures. Here, the raven figure is an embodiment of McMaster's bi-cultural heritage, a physical manifestation of duality, protected by the natural world that surrounds it.

The natural beauty and uncertainty of the environment plays a large role in many of the works from the *In-Between Worlds* series. In *Consanguinity*, the artist stands upon a rock before an endless body of water. While the subject is still, the water ripples and the plastic wrap cocoons the body through the force of the wind. The environment becomes a part of the performance, captured by the photograph.

Nature is constantly changing, as are personal perceptions. Works such as *Telltales* capture these fleeting moments—the blowing of ribbon and feathers attached to a makeshift mast, the placement of a foot in the snow, the bend of the body against a cold wind—all captured and preserved. A person changes from day to day, as does the environment. McMaster strives to capture these instances that inform her future.

In *Aphoristic Currents*, the environment becomes less of the subject. McMaster appears in the center of a coiled collar of newspapers.

This image features a large, exaggerated Victorian ruff made of carefully selected newsprint that represents language, technology, communication, information, and power in the past and present. The ruff also appears as flowing water or wind and my face is camouflaged in the likeness of the newspaper. The dots on my face represent the way the newspaper ink is applied to the paper.[11]

Now the emphasis is on the artist as a member of society, surrounded by media. This plethora of information encircles and absorbs

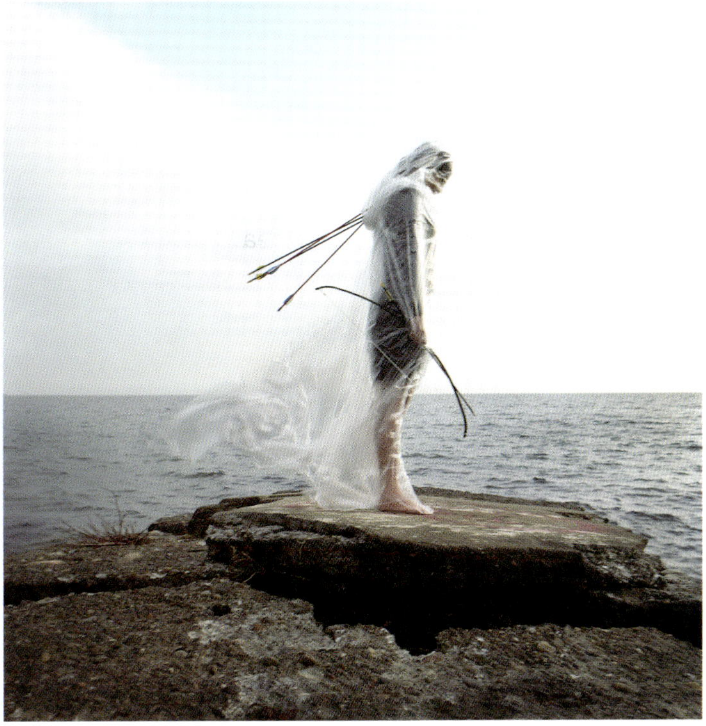

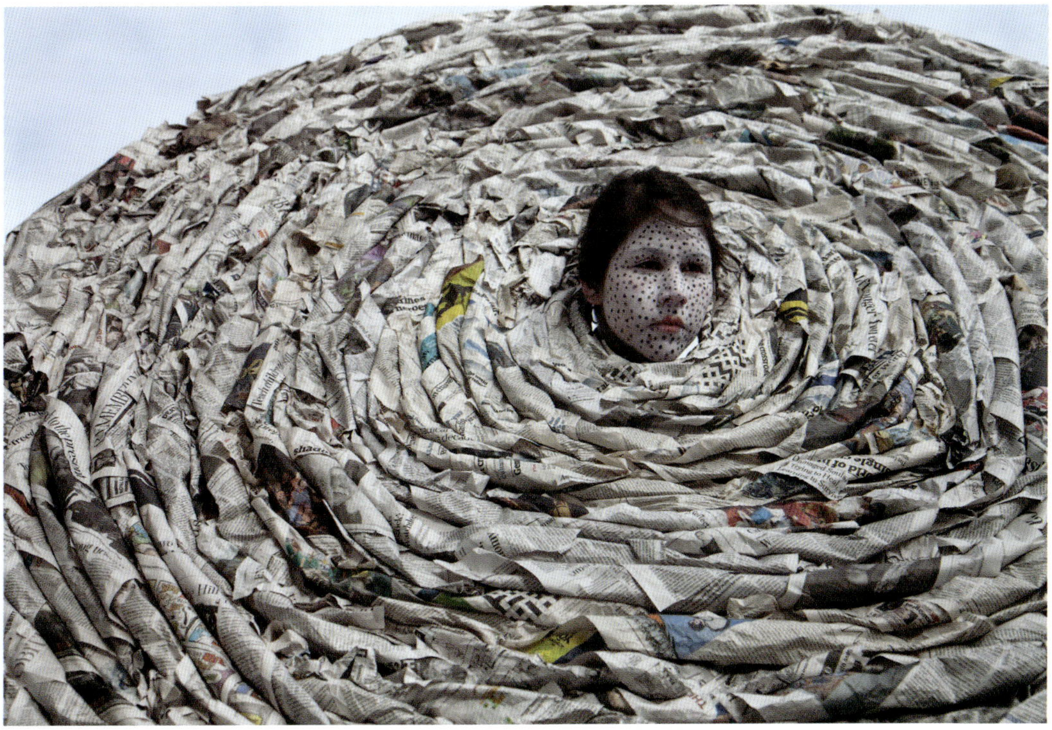

(Above) *Consanguinity (In-Between Worlds* series*)*, 2010. Digital chromogenic print. Image courtesy the artist. (Below) *Aphoristic Currents (In-Between Worlds* series*)*, 2013. Digital chromogenic print. Image courtesy the artist.

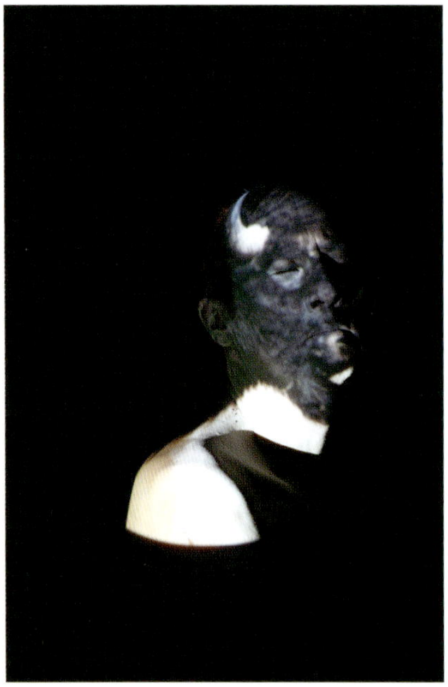
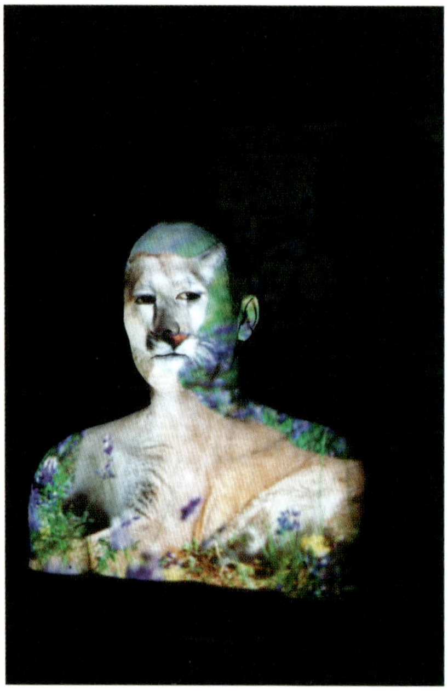
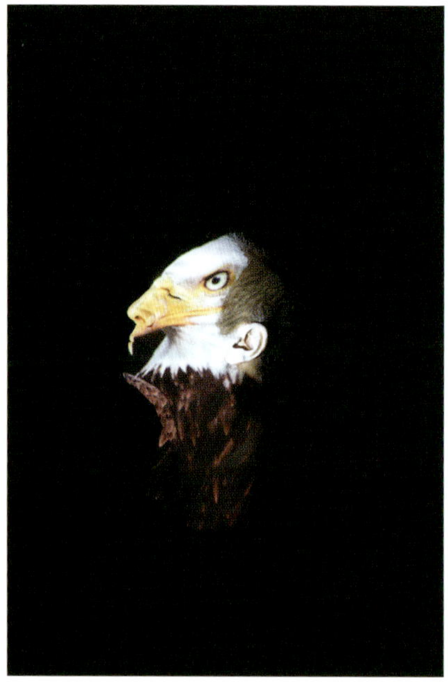
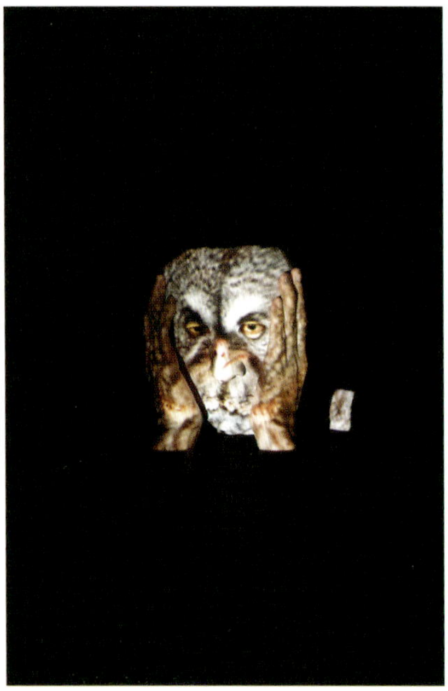
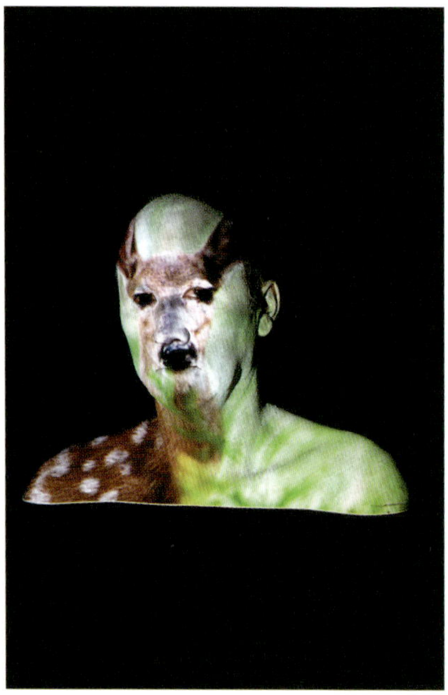
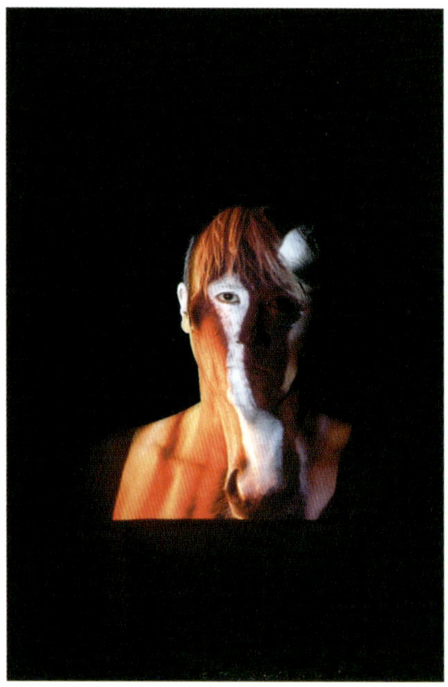

(Above, left to right) *Buffalo*; *Cougar*; *Eagle*. (Below, left to right) *Owl*; *Fawn*; *Horse (Ancestral* series*)*, 2010. Digital chromogenic print. Images courtesy the artist.

McMaster, to the point that she appears almost to be choked by it. Currently, we become engrossed by the news passed through the media; it consumes our existence. The sky that peeks over the newspapers is but a glimpse, a small part of the reality of a modern-day life that is far removed from nature.

The opposite can be said for the work *Anima*. Here, McMaster is engulfed by nature. *Anima* means "life" in Latin, and butterflies are often seen as the souls of aboriginal ancestors. The cold setting of winter and the pale skin of the artist is in stark contrast to the vibrant butterflies, which are full of life and movement. They descend upon McMaster, seeking out other life. The ancestors within the butterflies surround the artist, becoming a part of her in that moment.

Whereas the *In-Between Worlds* series is created by placing the subject, the artist, out in the world, the *Ancestral* series moves back to a more traditional studio portrait setting. McMaster wrestles with the lens of time. She is looking into the future or from the present into the past and exploring how this challenges perceptions and changes worldviews. *Ancestral*

> *explores the idea of heritage through a combination of portraits and self-portraits. Using late nineteenth-century historical images of various aboriginal men and women, the images were digitally projected onto the subject. The idea is to take historical bodies by inserting them into the present, bringing together old and new, as a way of looking at the past through the present.*[12]

Ancestral 1-16 shows a blending of old and new, two entities becoming one. The final product is a marriage of two separate and different people, but the result is a singular being that has absorbed features from both. The quest for self-realization and recognition that McMaster undertakes in her artwork is the narrative of an artist who is taking the viewer with her on her transformational journey.

It is within this series that McMaster first dealt with the aboriginal side of her identity. McMaster is purposeful in the images that she projects onto her subject. She appropriated historical images of aboriginal men and women by photographers Edward S. Curtis and Will Soule and paintings by

George Catlin, who painted portraits of Native peoples. All these artists were guilty of subscribing to the idea of a "vanishing race," which contended that documenting Native people was necessary so they would not be fully lost to history. The fault in that philosophy is, of course, that Native people were not vanishing but simply adapting to their environment. McMaster allows these romanticized relics of a manufactured history of the past to emerge into the present. Native people must still fight against these stereotypes, and the overlaying of the images helps show this struggle.

The later works in the *Ancestral* series take McMaster's exploration of her aboriginal identity a step farther. Again, the underlying image is a human study. However, now that role is being fulfilled by her father, who sat for some of the photographs. McMaster's father is in these moments the metaphorical and physical source of her aboriginal heritage. The projected images are no longer human but now are animals that are often associated with aboriginal people, such as buffalo and eagles. The human subject at times becomes almost completely absorbed into the animal image. At other times, the animal only intensifies the subject featured beneath it. The overall theme is to intensify the aboriginal identity, both from a personal level through the inclusion of the artist's father and a cultural level through the animals.

McMaster's duality of identity goes a step beyond bi-cultural heritage in the *Second Self* series. Here, issues of self-realization are internalized.

> *[The series] reconsiders portraiture by incorporating drawing and sculpture to evoke a world not normally seen by the naked eye. The thematic ideas of identity and masking led me to the concept of "persona." We invent personas—or social masks—through clothing, hairstyles, and posture, for example, and they have come to define the individual for the public while concealing the real person.*[13]

Each subject is painted in white, placed against stark black backgrounds. The racial marker of (often misleading) skin tone is completely removed. Most subjects stare directly at the camera, although a few have positioned themselves away or have shut one or both eyes. This is a very intimate and personal image. Unique sculptures made of a working of metal wires hang in front of each person. While this may at first be viewed as a barrier between the viewer and subject, that is hardly the case. Each seemingly random design of wires is actually a recreation of a self-portrait that the subject was asked to create. Using blind contour drawing, each subject has created a drawing of how he or she sees him- or herself. It is a double representation of portraiture: both the reality captured by the camera and the subject's self-perception. But both are edited, either through the use of the white paint or the limitations of blind contour drawing. The fact that each photograph is titled with the name of the subject contributes to the self-identity of the work. The *Second Self* series explores, experiments, and reconsiders identity(s) through portraiture by incorporating drawing and sculpture, the use of the mask as second self, and/or as an exploration of "double consciousness."

In *Becoming Laura*, a work that is unique because it is not part of a larger series, McMaster pays homage to Laura Ingersoll Secord, a distant relative, and her act of bravery during the War of 1812.

Shadows and text portray her journey as she makes the difficult decision to warn British soldiers and First Nation warriors of an impending American assault on Niagara and York. Assuming the form of Laura, I carry her tale on a symbol of the political and economic forces that led to this critical moment in Canadian history—a ship's sail. From this sail, words from the song "Secord's Warning" drift away as if calling out into the night in hopes of reaching her wounded husband's comrades on the Niagara Escarpment. Meanwhile, a messenger of "ill omen," the Raven, appears on my head to guide me/Laura through this ordeal. As history tells us, Laura's warning was given upon reaching the encampment, and the British and Mohawk allies met the American army two days later and were victorious.[14]

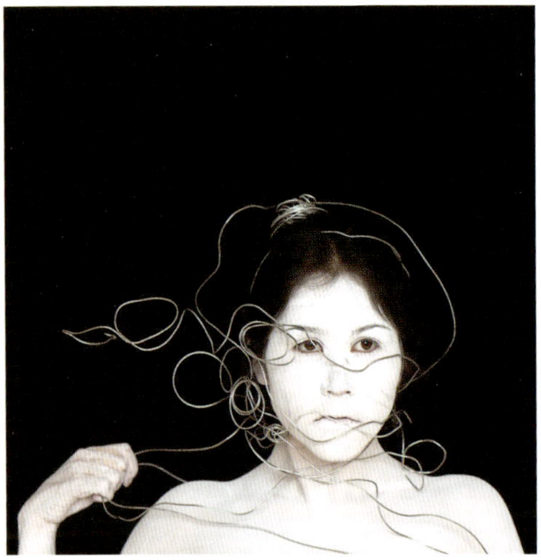

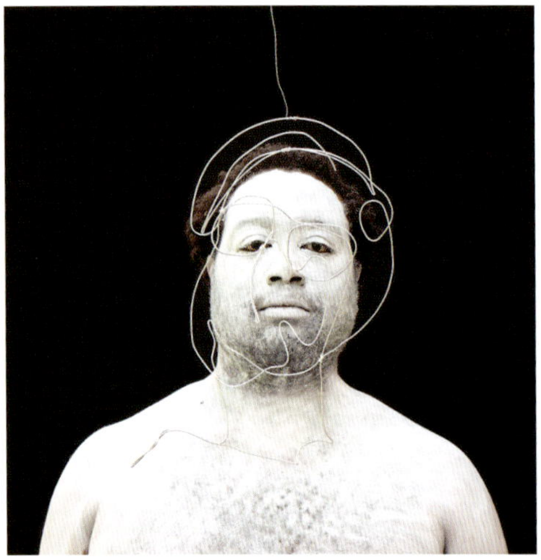

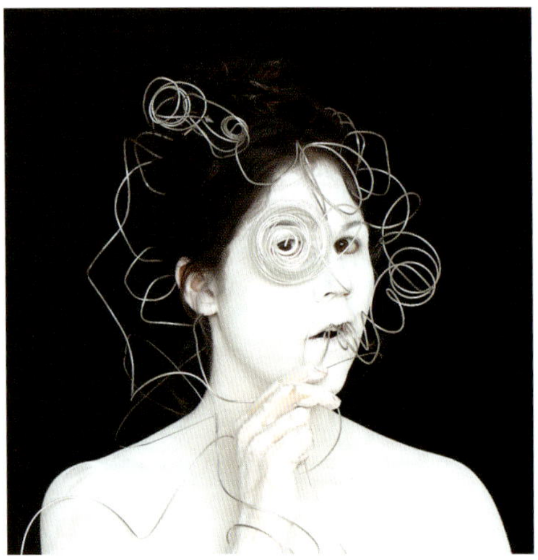

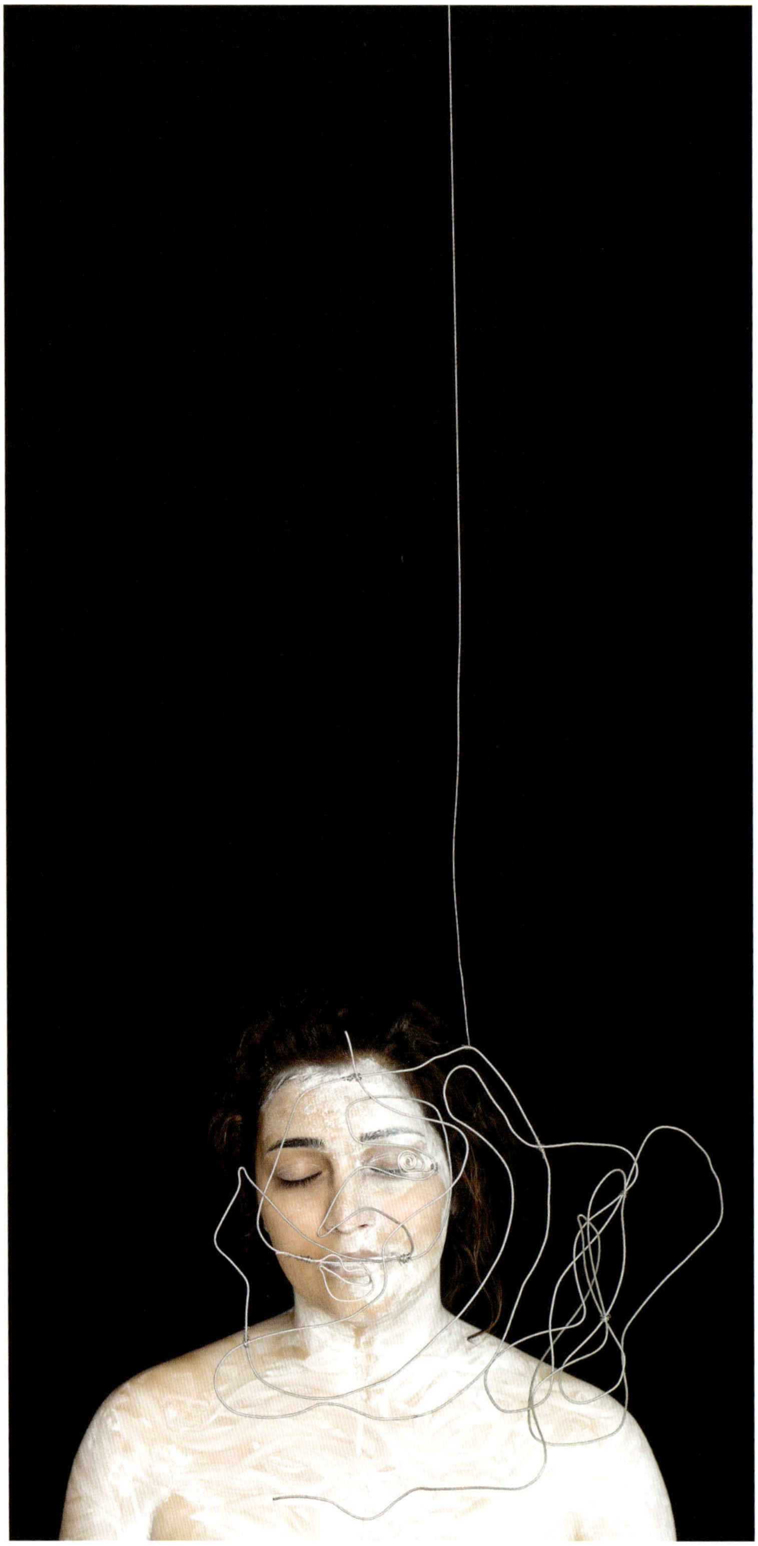

(Left, top to bottom) *Meryl 2*; *Anthony*; *Meryl 3*. (Right) *Nasrin (Second Self series)*, 2010. Digital chromogenic print. Images courtesy the artist.

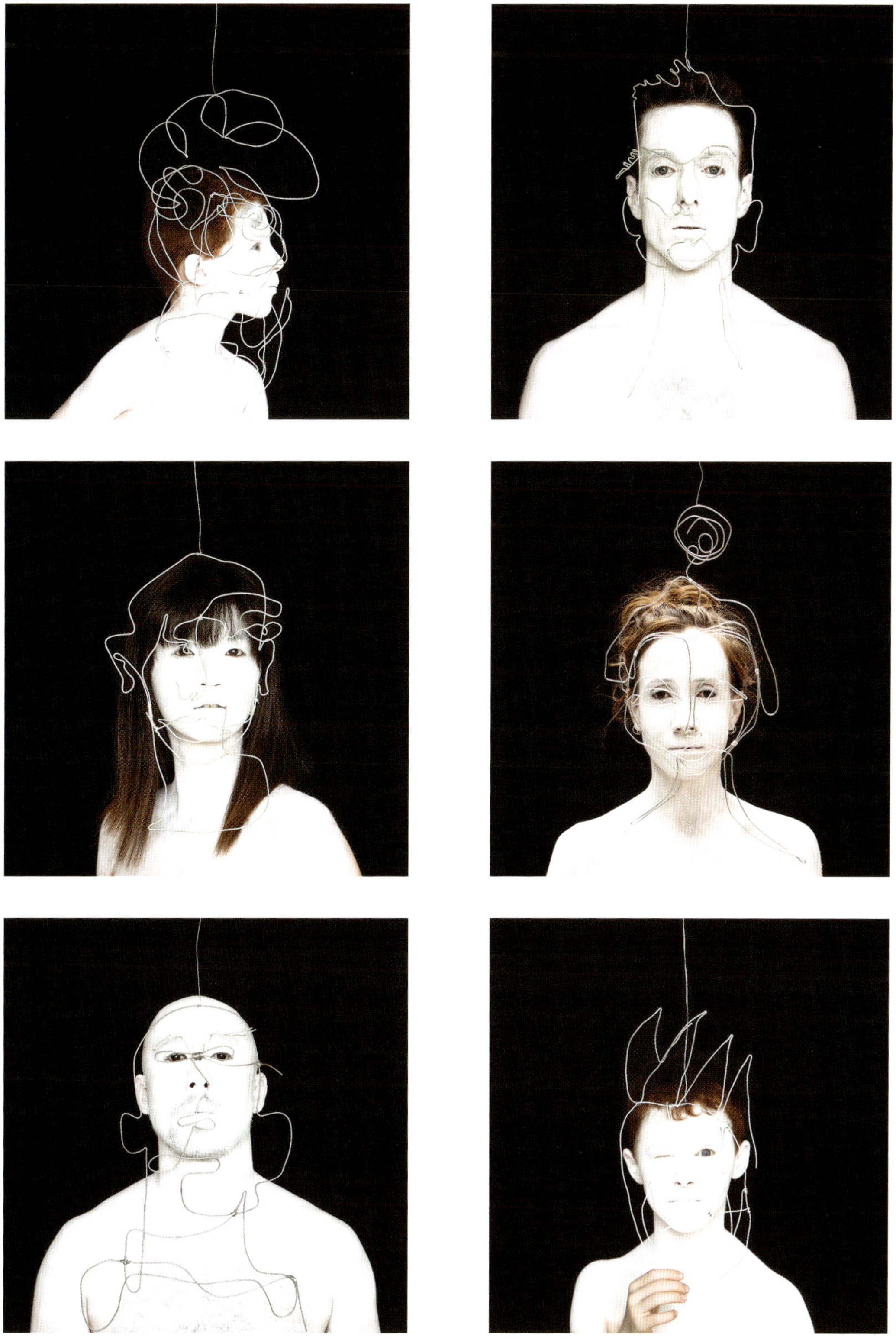

(Left, top to bottom) *Fred*; *Jin*; *Logan*, (Right, top to bottom) *Jordan*; *Pia*; *Jacob (Second Self* series*)*, 2010. Digital chromogenic print. Images courtesy the artist.

Once again, McMaster explores identity through her heritage. She takes on the persona of her relative, a hero of Canadian history for both Native and non-Natives, and gives narrative shape to her exploration and acceptance of a bi-cultural identity.

When McMaster's body of work is examined as a whole, it is hard to remember that she is still in the emerging stages of her career. Her artistic voice is strong, and there is a confidence in her visual expression that many artists strive decades to achieve. This strength comes from the reality of her process. McMaster never approaches a new work without deep consideration for the materials, the meaning, the expression, even the setting. She has a strong grasp on her bi-cultural heritage. She does not see struggle within this duality but allows for both sides to inform her work. The results are images that have multi-faceted meaning and depth. They speak to the viewer in a way that is highly personal. Looking at a photograph by McMaster is similar to the act of looking in the mirror, whether one is examining one's own reflection or that of someone else. The insight is intimate, uncensored, and often unnerving. McMaster invites this exploration of self. It is the very soul of her work.

---

[1]A portion of this essay was originally written by Jennifer Complo McNutt with the aid of research done by Betty Julian.

[2]The Idle No More movement began in 2012 as a peaceful public protest "to [honor] Indigenous sovereignty and to protect the land and water." More information can be found at www.idlenomore.ca.

[3]Meryl McMaster, "In-Between Worlds" (senior thesis, Ontario College of Art and Design, 2010), 2.

[4]Victor Turner, *The Ritual Process: Structure and Anti-structure* (Chicago: Aldine Publishing Co,1969), 95.

[5]McMaster, "In-Between Worlds," 2.

[6]Betty Julian, research notes, August 15, 2013.

[7]Meryl McMaster, interview with author, August 20, 2013.

[8]McMaster, "In-Between Worlds," 2.

[9]McMaster, "In-Between Worlds," 5–6.

[10]McMaster, interview with author, August 20, 2013.

[11]Ibid.

[12]"Meryl McMaster: Portfolio, Ancestral," accessed August 21, 2013, http://merylmcmaster.com/section/164673_Ancestral.html.

[13]Artist's statement for Eiteljorg Museum, Indianapolis, 2013.

[14]"Meryl McMaster: Portfolio, Becoming Laura," accessed August 21, 2013, http://merylmcmaster.com/section/301692_Becoming_Laura.html.

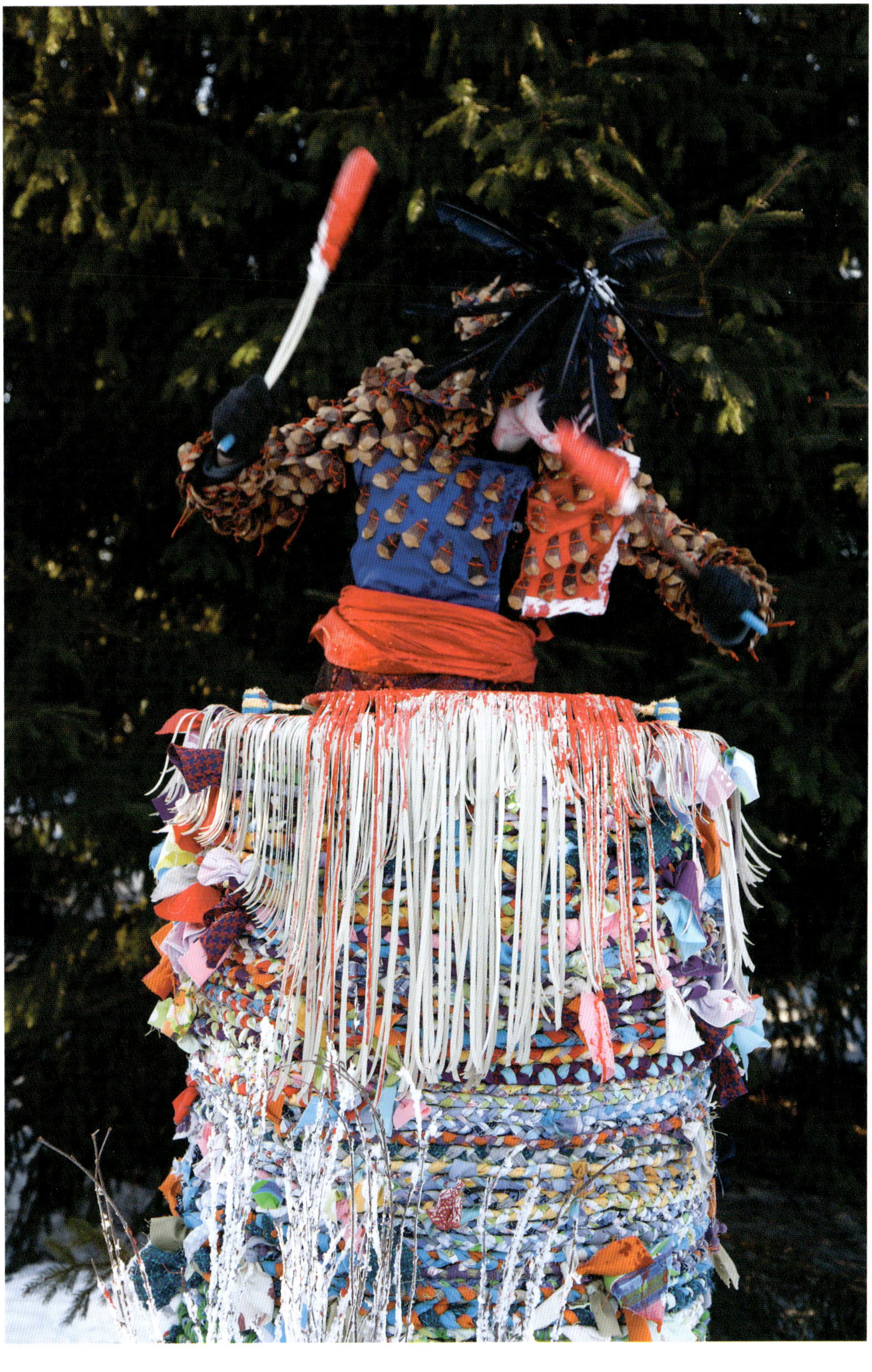

Brumal Tattoo (In-Between Worlds series*)*, 2013. Digital chromogenic print. Image courtesy the artist.

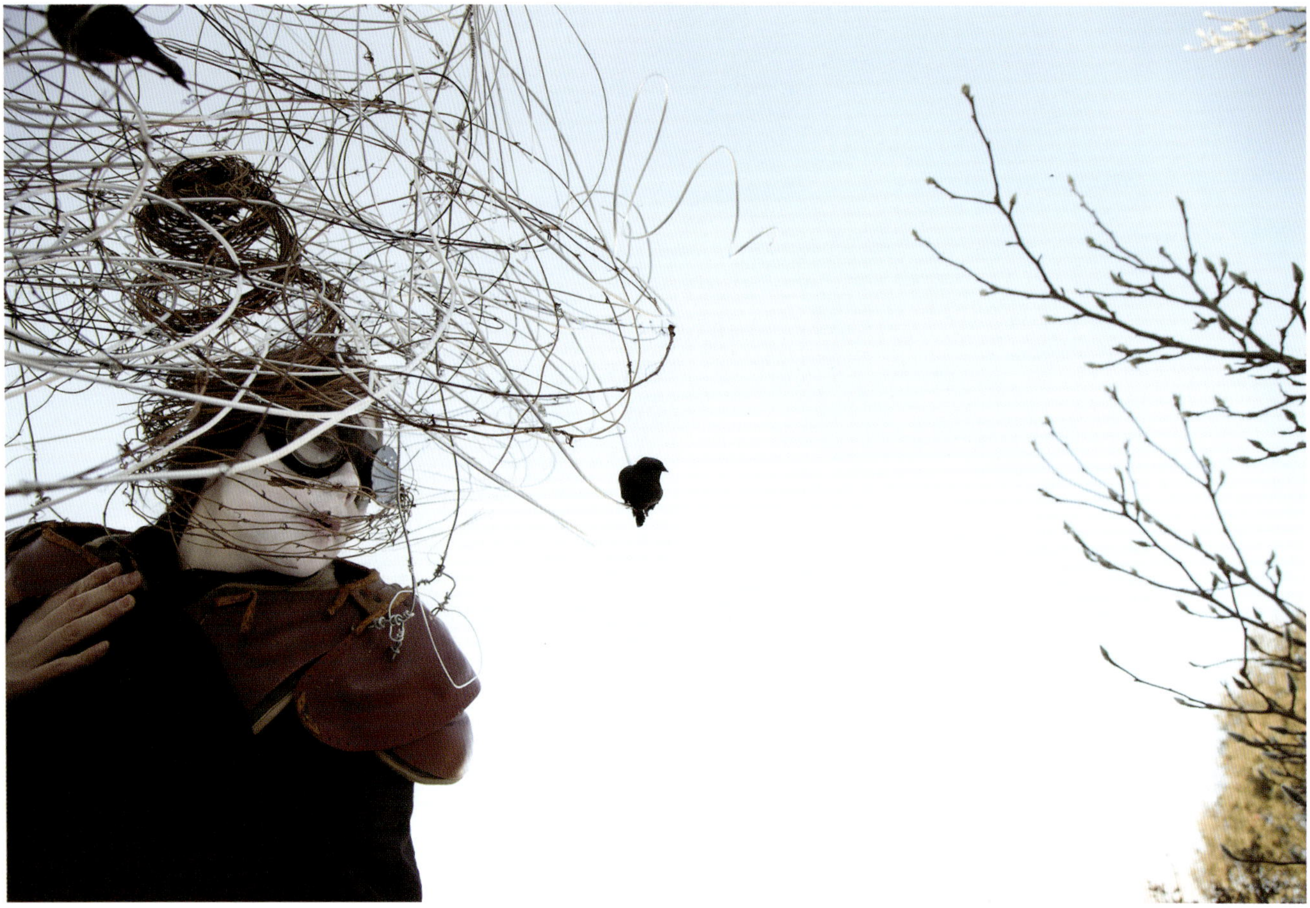

Harbinger of Sudden Departures (In-Between Worlds series), 2013. Digital chromogenic print. Image courtesy the artist.

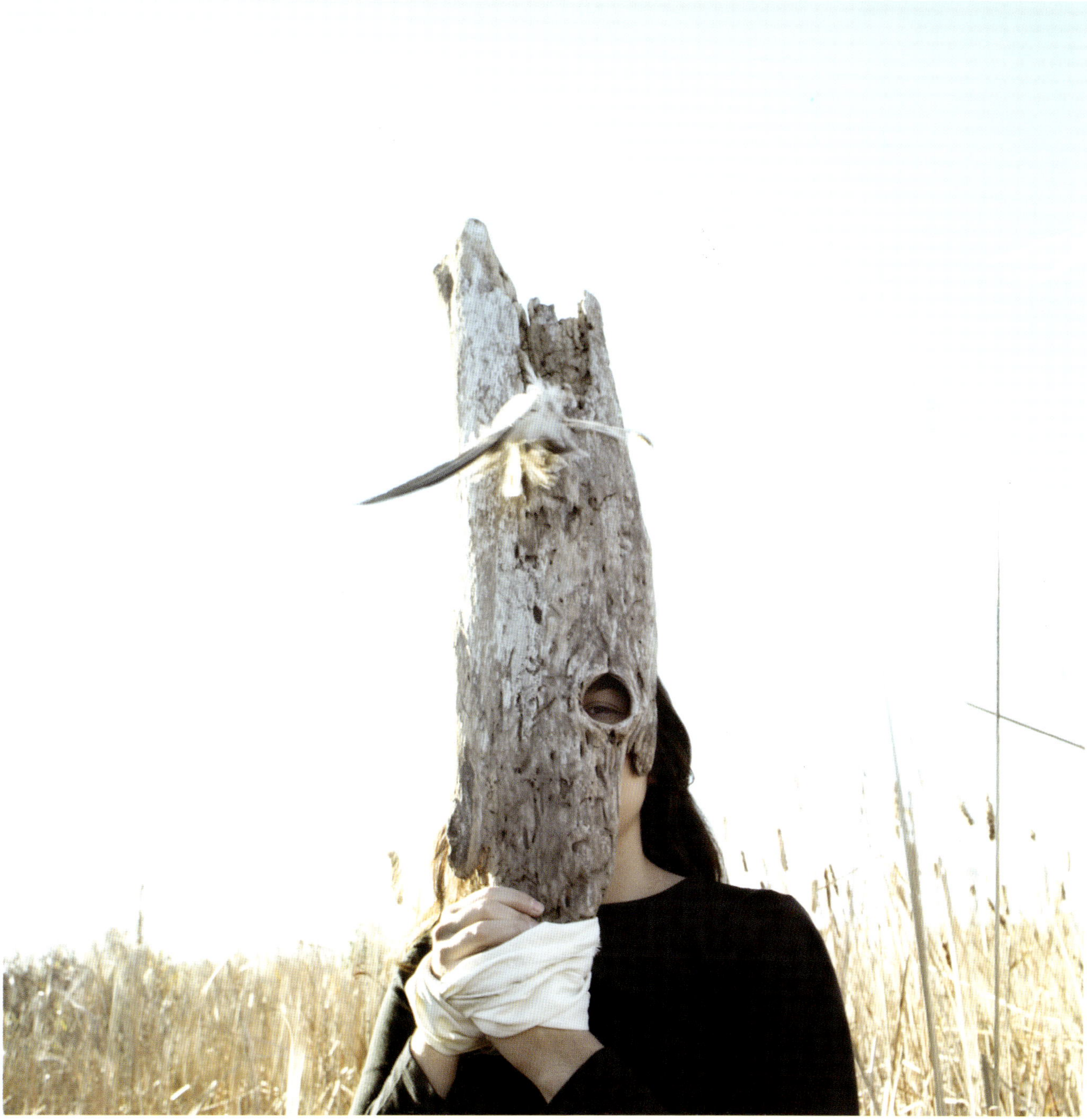

Tilsam (In-Between Worlds series*)*, 2010. Digital chromogenic print. Image courtesy the artist.

Checklist

Dimensions are given in inches, height by width by depth.

Lawrence Paul Yuxweluptun

(Coast Salish/Okanagan)

Black Ovoids in Deep Blue Sea, 2013
Acrylic on canvas
84 x 72
Eiteljorg Contemporary Art Fellowship Acquisition Fund

Caution! You Are Entering a Free State of Mind Zone, 2000
Acrylic on canvas
71 x 108
Private Collection

Clear Cut to the Last Tree, 1993
Screenprint, edition 6/98
32 x 22
Courtesy of Ken Stephens

The Direction of Land Claim Negotiations, 2013
Acrylic on canvas
68 x 72
Courtesy of Macaulay & Co. Fine Art

Floor Opener, 2013
Acrylic on canvas
76 x 96
Courtesy of Michael O'Brian

Fucking Creeps They're Environmental Terrorists, 2013
Acrylic on canvas
72 x 84
Courtesy of Macaulay & Co. Fine Art

Guardian Spirits on the Land: Ceremony on Sovereignty, 2000
Acrylic on canvas
72 x 98
Courtesy of Michael O'Brian

Indian World My Home and Native Land, 2012
Acrylic on canvas
120 x 84
Private Collection, Canada

The Last Old Growth Spirit Tree, 2012
Etching on St. Armand paper, edition 7/25
65 x 19
Eiteljorg Contemporary Art Fellowship Acquisition Fund

Losing Identities, 1999
Acrylic on canvas
81 x 52 inches
Courtesy of Michael O'Brian

The New Legend: The Screaming Liberal, Begging for a Referendum on Land Claims, 1999
Acrylic on canvas
71 x 48 inches
Courtesy of Michael O'Brian

One Night in the Forest, 1994
Pen on paper
30 x 22.5
Courtesy of Ken Stephens

Pole Raising, 2013
Acrylic on canvas
88 x 43.5
Courtesy of Macaulay & Co. Fine Art

Portrait of a Residential School Child, 2005
Acrylic on canvas
64 x 52.5 inches
Private Collection

Super Clear Cut, 1993
Etching, edition 5/90
39.5 x 28
Private Collection

Untitled, 1986
Pen and pencil on paper
13.5 x 10
Courtesy of Ken Stephens

Untitled, 1986
Pen and pencil on paper
13.5 x 10
Courtesy of Ken Stephens

Untitled, 2013
Pen on paper
10 x 7.25
Courtesy of Ken Stephens

Untitled (Figure), 1980–1995
Pen and watercolor on paper
12 x 10
Courtesy of Ken Stephens

Untitled (Figure), 1985
Pen and pencil on paper
10.5 x 8.5
Courtesy of Ken Stephens

Untitled (Figure), 1995
Pen and ink on paper
21.5 x 13.5
Courtesy of Ken Stephens

Untitled (Landscape), 1987
Pen on paper
13.5 x 10
Courtesy of Ken Stephens

Untitled (Longhouse Interior), date unknown
Pen and pencil on paper
13.5 x 21.5 inches
Courtesy of Ken Stephens

Untitled Portrait, 2003
Pen on paper
9 x 7
Courtesy of Ken Stephens

Untitled Portrait, 2003
Pen on paper
9 x 7
Courtesy of Ken Stephens

Untitled Portrait, 2003
Pen on paper
9 x 7
Courtesy of Ken Stephens

Untitled Portrait, 2003
Pen on paper
9 x 7
Courtesy of Ken Stephens

White Man Speaks with Forked Tongue, Land Claims Consultant I, 2013
Pen on paper
6.5 x 5.5
Courtesy of Ken Stephens

White Man Speaks with Forked Tongue, Land Claims Consultant II, 2013
Pen on paper
6.5 x 5.5
Courtesy of Ken Stephens

White Man Speaks with Forked Tongue, Land Claims Consultant III, 2013
Pen on paper
6.5 x 5.5
Courtesy of Ken Stephens

Ya Right Homie New Transformation Beep Beep Beep the Formline LOL, 2013
Acrylic on canvas
91 x 75
Courtesy of Macaulay & Co. Fine Art

Julie Buffalohead

(Ponca Tribe of Oklahoma)

The Columbus Prophecies, 2012
Mixed media on paper
20 x 30.5
Eiteljorg Contemporary Art Fellowship Acquisition Fund

The Confirmation, 2009
Mixed media on paper
20.5 x 30.5
Courtesy of National Museum of the American Indian, Smithsonian Institution

The Dog Paddle, 2012
Mixed media on paper
20 x 30
Eiteljorg Contemporary Art Fellowship Acquisition Fund

Fearsome Critter, 2012
Mixed media on paper
20 x 30
Eiteljorg Contemporary Art Fellowship Acquisition Fund

Heart Sick, 2012
Mixed media on paper
30 x 20
Eiteljorg Contemporary Art Fellowship Acquisition Fund

Hostage, 2008
Mixed media on paper
19 x 25
Courtesy of National Museum of the American Indian, Smithsonian Institution

I Feel This Much, 2009
Mixed media on paper
26.5 x 35.5
Courtesy of Wilson and Brenda Pipestem

Let the Show Begin, 2010
Mixed media on paper
19.5 x 25.5
Courtesy of National Museum of the American Indian, Smithsonian Institution

Little Boo Peep Forgot about her Sheep, 2012
Mixed media on paper
19.5 x 30
Courtesy of the artist and Bockley Gallery

The Little Glass Slipper, 2012
Mixed media on paper
20 x 30
Courtesy of Russell Cowles

The Lone Ranger Rides Again, 2012
Mixed media on paper
20 x 30
Courtesy of Mark Tierney

The Love Object, 2012
Mixed media on paper
20 x 15
Courtesy of Mira Alexander

The Medusa Syndrome, 2010
Mixed media on paper
20 x 30
Eiteljorg Contemporary Art Fellowship Acquisition Fund

My Life as Performed by Coyote, Rabbit, and Various Toys, 2012
Mixed media on paper
30.25 x 59
Courtesy of Judy Meath and Xandra Coe

Pillow Fight, 2012
Mixed media on paper
19.5 x 25.5
Courtesy of Ellen Miller and Daniel Shindelar

Reconcile, 2011
Mixed media on paper
30 x 20
Courtesy Dan Lindsey

Seems You Have to Play Indian to Be Indian, 2010
Mixed media on paper
18 x 20
Courtesy of National Museum of the American Indian, Smithsonian Institution

Sometimes the Magic Works, Sometimes It Doesn't, 2012
Mixed media on paper
26 x 34.5
Courtesy of Suzette and Michael Whitt

The Spirit Trees, 2010
Mixed media on paper
20 x 25.5
Courtesy of National Museum of the American Indian, Smithsonian Institution

The Standoff, 2012
Mixed media on paper
24.75 x 34.25
Courtesy of Thomas Arneson

Storyteller, 2008
Mixed media on paper
20 x 18
Courtesy of Julie Pace

Tea Party Day One, 2008
Mixed media on handmade paper
20 x 30
Courtesy of Marie Rizkalla

Tea Party Day Three, 2008
Mixed media on paper
20 x 30
Courtesy of the artist and Bockley Gallery

Warpaint, 2012
Mixed media on paper
19.5 x 30
Courtesy of Judy Meath and Xandra Coe

Nicholas Galanin

(Tlingit/Aleut)

The American Dream is Alie and Well, 2012
United States flag, felt, .50 caliber blank cartridges, foam, gold leaf, plastic
84 x 84 x 9
Courtesy of the artist

I Looooove Your Culture! Fine Wood Working, 2012
Yellow cedar
9.5 x 4 x 4
Courtesy of the artist

I Think It Goes Like This?, 2012
Wood, paint
Various dimensions
Eiteljorg Contemporary Art Fellowship Acquisition Fund

No Indians or Dogs Allowed, 2008
Neon, photography
Various dimensions
Courtesy of the Pratt Museum

U'háan-We, 2012 [in collaboration with Jerrod Galanin as Leonard Getinthecar]
Radio transmitter tuned to 93.7 broadcasting Tlingit language lessons, aluminum antenna, iPod shuffle, nineteenth-century Tlingit redcorner bentwood storage box
Various dimensions
Courtesy of the artist

Shan Goshorn

(Eastern Band of Cherokee)

39, 2012
Arches watercolor paper splints, first printed with archival inks
14.25 x 10.5 dia.
Eiteljorg Contemporary Art Fellowship Acquisition Fund

All They Could See in Blue Mountains Was Gold, 2012
Mixed media
13.5 x 15.5 dia.
Courtesy of Ari and Lea Plosker

Cherokee Burden Basket; Singing a Song for Balance, 2013
Archival watercolor paper splints, first printed with archival inks
24 x 19 dia.
Courtesy of the artist

Commodity Products, 2012
Archival watercolor paper splints, first printed with archival inks
5.875 x 5.5 x 5 (each)
Courtesy of the Minneapolis Institute of Arts, The Patricia and Peter Frechette Endowment for Art Acquisition

Despite (aka Three Sisters), 2012
Archival watercolor paper splints, first printed with archival inks
5.5 x 8.5 x 9
9 x 5 dia.
7 x 7 dia.
Courtesy of William and Brenda Pipestem

Double Crossed, 2013
Mixed media
4 x 2.5 dia.
Courtesy of the artist

Forever a Part of Us, 2012
Arches watercolor paper splints, first printed with archival inks
1.75 x 2.75 x 1.5
Courtesy of the artist

Forever Woven into Our Fabric, 2012
Archival watercolor paper splints, first printed with archival inks
12.25 x 16 dia.
Courtesy of the artist

Golden Rule, Overruled, 2013
Mixed media
3.25 x 2.25 dia.
Courtesy of the artist

Gold Exchanged, 2013
Mixed media
2.75 x 2.75 dia.
Courtesy of the artist

It's Not Just Black and White, 2013
Mixed media
4 x 3.5 dia.
Courtesy of the collection of B and B Harjo

On the Shoulders of a Child, 2013
Mixed media
3 x 3 dia.
Courtesy of the artist

Pieced Treaties; Spider's Web Treaty Basket, 2008
Arches watercolor paper splints, first printed with archival inks
28 x 20 dia.
Courtesy of National Museum of the American Indian, Smithsonian Institution

Removal (Ancestral Homeland) and *Removal (Indian Territory)*, 2012
Mixed media
13 x 12 dia. (each)
Courtesy of the artist

Separating the Chaff, 2013
Archival watercolor paper splints, first printed with archival inks
7 x 18 dia.
Courtesy of Fred Jones Jr. Museum of Art, University of Oklahoma

So Long as These Waters Run, 2012
Arches watercolor paper splints, first printed with archival inks
12.5 x 8 dia.
Courtesy of the artist

Theological Discussion, 2013
Mixed media
4.25 x 2.5 dia.
Courtesy of the artist

Turned a Blind Eye, 2013
Mixed media
4.5 x 2.875 dia.
Courtesy of David and Sarah Lieberman

Underhanded Allies, 2013
Mixed media
4 x 2.75 dia.
Courtesy of the artist

Unsolicited Gifts or How to Eliminate a Culture, 2012
Archival watercolor paper splints, first printed with archival inks
6.5 x 14 x 11
Courtesy of the artist

Windwoven, 2013
Acrylic on canvas
60 x 72
Courtesy of the artist

Meryl McMaster

(Plains Cree/Blackfoot)

Anima (In-Between Worlds series*)*, 2012
Digital chromogenic print
36 x 36
Eiteljorg Contemporary Art Fellowship Acquisition Fund

Anthony (Second Self series*)*, 2010
Digital chromogenic print
36 x 36
Courtesy of the artist

Aphoristic Currents (In-Between Worlds series*)*, 2013
Digital chromogenic print
36 x 50.3
Eiteljorg Contemporary Art Fellowship Acquisition Fund

Brumal Tattoo (In-Between Worlds series*)*, 2013
Digital chromogenic print
50.3 x 36
Courtesy of the artist

Buffalo (Ancestral series*)*, 2010
Digital chromogenic print
40 x 30
Courtesy of the artist

Caduceus (In-Between Worlds series*)*, 2010
Digital chromogenic print
24 x 24
Courtesy of the artist

Consanguinity (In-Between Worlds series*)*, 2010
Digital chromogenic print
24 x 24
Courtesy of the artist

Cougar (Ancestral series*)*, 2010
Digital chromogenic print
40 x 30
Courtesy of the artist

Eagle (Ancestral series*)*, 2010
Digital chromogenic print
40 x 30
Courtesy of the artist

Fawn (Ancestral series*)*, 2010
Digital chromogenic print
40 x 30
Courtesy of the artist

Fred (Second Self series*)*, 2010
Digital chromogenic print
36 x 36
Courtesy of the artist

Harbinger of Sudden Departures (In-Between Worlds series*)*, 2013
Digital chromogenic print
36 x 50.3
Courtesy of the artist

Horse (Ancestral series*)*, 2010
Digital chromogenic print
40 x 30
Courtesy of the artist

Jacob (Second Self series*)*, 2010
Digital chromogenic print
36 x 36
Courtesy of the artist

Jin (Second Self series*)*, 2010
Digital chromogenic print
36 x 36
Courtesy of the artist

Jordan (Second Self series*)*, 2010
Digital chromogenic print
36 x 36
Courtesy of the artist

Logan (Second Self series*)*, 2010
Digital chromogenic print
36 x 36
Courtesy of the artist

Meryl 2 (Second Self series*)*, 2010
Digital chromogenic print
36 x 36
Courtesy of the artist

Meryl 3 (Second Self series*)*, 2011
Digital chromogenic print
36 x 36
Courtesy of the artist

Nasrin (Second Self series*)*, 2010
Digital chromogenic print
72 x 36
Courtesy of the artist

Owl (Ancestral series*)*, 2010
Digital chromogenic print
40 x 30
Courtesy of the artist

Pia (Second Self series*)*, 2010
Digital chromogenic print
36 x 36
Courtesy of the artist

Sentience (In-Between Worlds series*)*, 2010
Digital chromogenic print
24 x 24
Courtesy of the artist

Terra Cognitum (In-Between Worlds series*)*, 2013
Digital chromogenic print
36 x 50.3
Courtesy of the artist

Tilsam (In-Between Worlds series*)*, 2010
Digital chromogenic print
24 x 24
Courtesy of the artist

Viage (In-Between Worlds series*)*, 2010
Digital chromogenic print
24 x 24
Courtesy of the artist

Victoria (In-Between Worlds series*)*, 2013
Digital chromogenic print
50.3 x 36
Courtesy of the artist

Wind Play (In-Between Worlds series*)*, 2012
Digital chromogenic print
36 x 36
Eiteljorg Contemporary Art Fellowship Acquisition Fund

Wingeds Calling (In-Between Worlds series*)*, 2012
Digital chromogenic print
36 x 50.3
Eiteljorg Contemporary Art Fellowship Acquisition Fund

Acknowledgments

It takes the combined energy and cooperation of many individuals to mount the Eiteljorg Contemporary Art Fellowship. The efforts of our patrons, lenders, contributors, staff, and visitors cannot be understated. It is my pleasure to acknowledge the contributions made by all to this year's exhibition.

This year, we have an extraordinary number of lenders to the exhibition. It is gratifying to work with such visionary individuals with such wonderful eyes. Your generous spirit and commitment to contemporary Native artists is inspiring to those of us who believe so strongly in their work. Please let me extend my personal gratitude to you all. Museum projects could not be done as well without your support.

Many collections are started and encouraged by the vision and commitment of galleries and their owners. Sarah Macaulay is one such owner. Sarah has introduced the museum to significant collections and collectors and coordinated communication that has contributed greatly to the success of this exhibition and the presentation of Lawrence Paul Yuxweluptun's work. Not to be outdone, Todd Bockley, owner of the Bockley Gallery in Minneapolis, is an advocate of several Native American artists (many former or current Eiteljorg Fellows) and this year supports the work of his 2013 Fellow, Julie Buffalohead. He too was instrumental in amassing work from collectors he and Julie have cultivated. Thank you, Sarah and Todd, for your thoughtful and patient work to ensure a presentation worthy of the artists you represent.

Once again, we express our gratitude to Suzanne G. Fox with Red Bird Publishing for her hard work on yet another luscious catalogue. Is this the sixth time already?! Speaking of old friends, Dirk Bakker and Giovanni Santitate have again provided professional and impeccable images for this publication. There was also the addition of Tad Fruits, who stepped in to take additional images to complete our photography for the catalogue. We extend a heartfelt thank you to Jean Christensen, of Arlington, Virginia, for her skillful copy editing of parts of this manuscript. This year, there is a new contributor to the creation of our catalog although he is a veteran at designing and mounting Fellowship. Steve Sipe, the Eiteljorg's director of exhibition and graphic design, has designed this publication. Thank you for an enjoyable working experience and a fresh approach to the catalogue.

What is a publication without writers? It is always a pleasure to work with those who provide a new interpretation of an artist's work. Placing the artists in context is critical, and we extend thanks and congratulations on their insightful and professional contributions to heather ahtone, Dana Claxton, and Tania Willard.

The exhibition is a manifestation of its visionary artists. Great appreciation goes to Lawrence Paul Yuxweluptun (Coast Salish/Okanagan), the 2013 Invited Artist, and the 2013 Fellows: Julie Buffalohead (Ponca Tribe of Oklahoma), Nicholas Galanin (Tlingit/Aleut), Shan Goshorn (Eastern Band of Cherokee), and Meryl McMaster (Plains Cree/Blackfoot).

The Eiteljorg staff has put tremendous effort and pride into this exhibition and publication, and it shows. Special thanks go to the collections staff for making all the shipping, moving, and photography efforts a success. That means you, Amy Mckune, director of museum collections, and our new registrar Christa Barleben!

My sincere thanks to Ashley Holland, assistant curator of contemporary art, whose organization and creativity are at the heart of the project. And again I thank James H. Nottage, vice president and chief curatorial officer, and John Vanausdall, president and CEO, for their patience and commitment to Native contemporary art, especially as it manifests in the 2013 Eiteljorg Fellowship.

It is impossible to single out every generous act by our staff members. Development, education, public programs, marketing, facilities, front-line staff, volunteers, and guides all carry the charge of helping to make this effort a success. I extend my undying gratitude to you all—no kidding.

Jennifer Complo McNutt, Curator of Contemporary Art
Eiteljorg Museum of American Indians and Western Art

Authors' Biographies

heather ahtone (Chickasaw Nation and Choctaw Nation of Oklahoma) is the James T. Bialac Assistant Curator for Native American and Non-Western Art at Fred Jones Jr. Museum of Art, University of Oklahoma, in Norman, Oklahoma. She holds a bachelor of fine arts degree and a master of arts degree from the University of Oklahoma and studied contemporary art history at the doctoral level at the University of Kansas. She has curated and co-curated many exhibitions, including *Edge Art Now* and *H2OK: Native Response to Water Issues in Oklahoma*. She has taught in the School of Art and Art History at the University of Oklahoma and served as associate editor of *International Journal of Arts in Society*. She has published widely and made many presentations at conferences and professional meetings.

Through her art practices, **Dana Claxton** (Lakota) has critiqued many aspects of government, religion, and consumer culture as they affect and disaffect contemporary aboriginal peoples in Canada and the United States. She has produced numerous single-channel works, video installations, and performances in the past decade. Taken together, these projects form a subversive societal critique in time-based media that suit experimental storytelling. She completed a master of arts degree in liberal studies from Simon Fraser University. Claxton received an Eiteljorg Contemporary Art Fellowship (formerly the Eiteljorg Fellowship for Native American Fine Art) in 2007. Her artwork is in the permanent art collections of many institutions across Canada, including the Canada Council Art Bank, Vancouver Art Gallery, Winnipeg Art Gallery, and numerous library collections.

Ashley Holland (Cherokee) is the assistant curator of contemporary art at the Eiteljorg Museum. She received her bachelor of arts in art history and religious studies from DePauw University in Greencastle, Indiana and her master of arts in museum studies with a scholarly emphasis on contemporary Native art and exhibition from Indiana University-Purdue University, Indianapolis. Holland has co-curated the Eiteljorg Contemporary Art

Fellowship since 2007. She also participates in the curation of the museum's permanent contemporary art collection and project management of temporary exhibitions and programs. She recently assisted in the presentation of a film series that examined past portrayals of Native peoples in the context of more modern, urban perspectives on Native life and self-images.

Jennifer Complo McNutt is the curator of contemporary art for the Eiteljorg Museum and has been instrumental in the development and success of the Eiteljorg Contemporary Art Fellowship since its inception in 1999. McNutt has curated more than forty exhibitions and contributed to numerous publications over her twenty-two year tenure at the Eiteljorg. She holds a bachelor of fine arts degree from Indiana University, Bloomington, and a master of fine arts degree from Tyler School of Art, Temple University, in Philadelphia. McNutt serves the arts community nationally and regionally as a selector, contributor, presenter, and advocate for Native contemporary art. She is currently leading a collaboration on a Eiteljorg publication exploring Native contemporary art from 1992 to the present.

Tania Willard (Secwepemc Nation) works within the shifting ideas around contemporary and traditional, often with knowledge and skills that are conceptually linked to her interest in intersections between aboriginal and other cultures. Willard has worked as an artist in residence at Gallery Gachet in Vancouver's Downtown East Side, the Banff Centre's visual arts residency, and as a curator in residence at Grunt Gallery. Her work is in the collections of the Department of Foreign Affairs and International Trade, Kamloops Art Gallery, and Thompson Rivers University. Willard's recent curatorial work includes *Beat Nation: Art Hip Hop and Aboriginal Culture*, co-curated with Kathleen Ritter, Vancouver Art Gallery, and featuring twenty-seven contemporary aboriginal artists.

Index